The

PRACTICE

GETTING
OUT OF YOUR
OWN WAY
Getting Out of Your Own Way LLC
11860 Clifton Blvd.

Lakewood, OH 44107

www.DrKeithJordan.com

Cover and layout design by *the*BookDesigners

ISBN: 978-0-0-9847937-0-9

Library of Congress Control Number: 2011943019

The

PRACTICE

Dr. Keith Jordan

GETTING
OUT OF YOUR
OWN WAY

11860 Clifton Blvd.
Lakewood, OH 44107

ONE DAY, I SAID . . .

"God, I've learned so much from my patients, my prayer, and my study, that I want to write a book about you."

"Don't write a book about me, Keith. Too many of them already," God said. "Write a book about Life instead. People don't connect me with their ordinary, every-day lives. They think I'm somehow outside their lives. They don't get that I am Life, Keith."

"It has to be a different kind of book," I said.

God said. "I know, Keith, show people how to practice living fully and loving their lives unconditionally. That's how they'll honor me most. . . . And begin to see my undeniable presence in their lives.

I'll help you."

CONTENTS

PREFACE

Dear Reader,

I want to introduce you to an inspired work that will take you on a journey into oneness with all of Life, all that has ever been and all that will ever be. Ceremonies of introduction are traditional, but the ceremony I propose here is simple: Take *The Practice* into your hands and begin to live Life more fully and joyfully than you ever have before.

The Practice is a series of inspired spiritual teachings that show your infinite soul how to live eternally. It's a simple book that everyone can learn from if you are ready, or desire to be ready, to grow in consciousness. If you still feel resistant to growing in consciousness, *The Practice* will help remove that resistance. As you experience Life in a way that brings deep prolonged states of peace, love, acceptance, and compassion, your resistance will ebb away, and you will discover the freedom of telling the truth and the joy that comes from balancing your body, mind, and spirit.

The Practice reminds you of universal truths especially about your primary relationship with Life. As you practice living intuitively, the energy of ego then surrenders into oneness with all of Life. All your choices dissolve into choice-less surrender. More and more, you focus on choosing moment by moment what is in the highest good, practicing love, acceptance, peace, and compassion. You will strengthen your relationship with Life as you become aware of the incredible order of Life, and the divinity behind it.

I welcome those with a heart open to love and a mind willing to change to join me on this journey into *The Practice*!

I love Life, with all that I am.
Keith

1.
LET'S BEGIN!

FULLY LIVING AND unconditionally loving your life is simple—especially if you become a student of Life, curious about what Life wants to teach you. That's how I discovered what I call *The Practice*; I became intrigued by Life and the more I studied it, the more intrigued I became. If you too became its student, you would likely come to the same conclusion: living fully and loving your life every moment is simple. There can be no higher goal for any being than to live in a space of unconditional love, acceptance, peace, and compassion forever. It is the reason for Life, the common purpose we all share, the reason we *are*. Isn't it good news that it's simple?

But usually, we don't think of Life as simple. We've gotten into the unfortunate habit of trying to "figure it out." We make Life into a problem. We struggle with Life, wrestle with it as if it were an enemy. We expect things of it—and find ourselves frequently disappointed. We complain that "Life is not fair." We even curse Life.

Rarely do we take the time to really look at what Life is and what Life isn't. When we study Life, when we look at Life through Life's eye, we find a partner not an enemy. But we are so busy reacting to Life instead of looking closely. I've come to realize that Life is our first, foremost, and *eternal* partner; it will always be with us. So why not learn to love it, learn how it wants to be loved, just as you would a lover?

When we see Life as our eternal partner and begin to practice loving her, being honest with her, being truthful with ourselves, we will begin to love Life unconditionally, no matter what. *No matter what.* When we stop reacting and struggling, Life moves towards us as a guide. As you move more deeply into *The Practice*, you will find it more and more simple to live fully and love Life unconditionally. I didn't always believe this, but now I do: Now I know that Life can be synonymous with peace. There is an inherent divine order to Life that becomes visible and awe-inspiring. It brings us peace.

This peace and unconditional love for our lives—no matter what—is available to each of us when we become ready to let go of the ingrained and habituated views about Life that we've probably believed for most of our lives. Society, religions, institutions, and popular culture, have put their opinions out there and we've accepted them as true. Yet, they are only opinions, only particular views. They are not the whole truth about Life. I've discovered that Life has some eternal and infinite truths—not

opinions—that serious students of Life come to realize. These truths are not new. Many spiritual masters
have written about them, including Jesus, the Buddha,
Mohammed, among others. But because Life's truths do
not fit with the ordinary opinions of the masses, they are
not recognized as truths.

Have you noticed, for example, that we don't really
have a choice about Life? We are *of* Life whether we want
to be or not. This is a truth. We are just one of many in the
field of Life that includes other people, animals, plants,
minerals, galaxies, suns and moons, stars, mosquitoes,
and lightning bugs. We were part of Life before we came
here in human form, we are part of Life now in all its
manifestations and, when we die, we still will be a part
of Life in one form or another. You could say that we *are*
Life, eternally.

When you begin to open to these truths and let go of
the ingrained opinions about Life, including your own
opinions, Life itself will teach you. I think of it as "getting
out of your own way." When we get out of our own way,
Life becomes our teacher, and we finally notice and appreciate Life's amazing divinity and perfection.

We will never understand Life in its totality. Yet we
can, with practice, allow Life to be the Great Master that
teaches us, eternally. If you do this, suddenly peace and
love take up all the space within you and joy becomes
your companion. You cease struggling with Life because
now you've let go and become its student. Life responds
by assisting you, guiding you, leading you.

Since Life is an eternal process, we can start where we are, let Life guide us, and go from there. This *is* a choice we have in this moment—to begin to look at Life and listen to it—rather than always fighting it. At some point, if we don't make the only choice we can make, Life will make it for us.

Our culture and religious systems have proposed that we are in control. But another truth I've learned is that Life has all the choices. The idea that we have personal choice is an illusion—except on a very superficial level, as any student of Life will come to recognize. I'll examine this idea more in the following chapters, but let's accept for now that we are not in control of Life. As you delve deeper into *The Practice*, you will come to realize, as I did, that Life will dictate all your relative decisions—you decide only how you will experience them—leaving you with only the immaterial illusion of personal choice.

While not having personal choice may sound like bad news, it helped me suddenly grasp and better understand my part in the field of Life. Allowing Life to decide, I've discovered, is really the better choice. As you grow in *The Practice*, you too will recognize that you are *of* Life and that Life is moving and directing you as you get out of your own way. As you surrender to Life, it will take you on a journey to your greatest and highest good.

Will that mean Life will always be good? Yes. Will you always understand why Life is good? Absolutely not! Yet another truth about Life that I've learned is that something that happens today—whether you like it or not—may have happened to actually heal something that took place ten years ago or ten lifetimes ago. Life is energy, after all, and energy is not limited by time or space. Or another possibility is that the situation—whether you label it as "good" or "bad"—may be preparing you, making you ready for something that will happen ten minutes, ten years, or ten lifetimes from now. We get caught up in judging Life's hiccups on a moment to moment basis; Life's funny or sad or troublesome moments confuse and worry us. But judging "moments" is akin to holding the tail of an elephant and then proposing that the animal is small and skinny.

We cannot begin to comprehend the complexity of Life at its truest level by evaluating individual moments with our senses and passing judgment on them. Instead, we can begin to look at Life through Life's eye. The next chapter will explain how to look at Life this way. But here's an example of seeing through Life's eye to set the stage.

Suppose you are fired from a job in which you are poorly paid and overworked. Nevertheless, you believe you need this job, you depend on it, and you're devastated that you've been fired. Maybe being fired from a job has happened to you before and now it's happening again. Maybe you have a history of being treated poorly both in your work life and your personal life. Perhaps even your parents were abusive in some way.

From Life's viewpoint, being fired is Life offering you another opportunity to grow in self-respect, worthiness, confidence, courage, and self-love. Suddenly, you have to come to terms with what is *eating* you on the inside, which has appeared outside in the form of a firing. You view such a thing as "terrible".

Life doesn't see it that way. Life wonders *Will she get it this time? Will she demand more respect? Or will she agree again to be underpaid and overworked? Will he learn this time to appreciate his own worth? Will he speak up on his own behalf? Will he develop courage?*

Life was delivering you from the tragedy of being underpaid, overworked, and mistreated. This is an example of how Life sees such situations.

Of course, you can always go on feeling abused without looking at the inner demon that is eating you alive. You can always accept another job in which you are underpaid, overworked, and mistreated.

Yet, in its loving way, Life will keep providing opportunities for us to learn. Circumstances happen to bring about the necessary changes that we ourselves are not bringing about. Life wants us to love ourselves and treat ourselves and others with respect. It wants us to be our highest, best, most courageous selves.

You never know what else might eventually happen based on your firing; perhaps ten minutes, ten months, ten years, or ten lifetimes from now someone might suddenly get an insight or some necessary and good thing might take place that provides you or someone else with an opportunity to grow, to thrive, to learn, to love. Life's intention in the long run is not something we can know— but it is always for the best. That's the only reason Life would allow something like a firing.

The Practice will bring you more deeply into a space of truth, joy, acceptance, and unconditional love with all of Life. You will move from opinion to truth, from hope to knowing, from confusion to deeper understanding, from fear to surrender, and from surrender to unconditional love, acceptance, and peace.

With hearts open to love and minds willing to learn, let's journey deeper into *The Practice* of living.

∽ 2. ∾

NAVIGATING LIFE
INTUITIVELY

LISTENING TO YOUR intuition is a key to loving Life unconditionally. It's the way that we, in our physical form, are able to look at Life through Life's eye. Learning to navigate Life intuitively is a critical piece if you desire to live in a space of deep peace.

Intuition is the sense that infinite truth is available to us in any situation. It is a knowing about what response is just, righteous, and of the highest good. It is also an accumulation of wisdom learned from Life and a deep awareness of Life's order in spite of any chaos we may see.

Each of us has intuition but we use it to a greater or lesser degree. Intuition has been called "the still small voice," "clear seeing," "looking with the third eye," "enlightened awareness," "conscious awareness," and "our higher center." The tiny pineal gland deep in our brain is sometimes aligned with the Third Eye, which, in yoga, is the seat of intuition. It's also been called "second sight." Learning to heighten our intuition is a great help in seeing Life clearly.

For the most part, we have become use to relying on our senses to interpret what is happening. I used to be a sensor, using sight, smell, taste, touch, and hearing to make sense of Life. Our five senses are important gifts, but they aren't the only gift we've been given to aid us in interpreting Life. Perhaps you haven't even thought about unwrapping the gift of intuition you were born with. When we use only our senses to understand Life, we use only one of the gifts we've been given. When Life put me in its classroom and I studied, I learned to develop my intuition. Now I can look at Life with both gifts.

For many of you, it may have become a habit to react to situations based on what your senses tell you. Our senses have a sort of cellular memory so that if you see a loving couple, up comes an emotion, such as sadness, along with *Remember when so-and so did that to you?* If you hear a certain song, an emotion arises along with *I wish she hadn't left me.* Living by your senses can trigger past memories— they do it all the time. What happened to our mothers while we were *in utero* happened to us because we felt our mother's reactions to something negative or positive that her senses experienced. Our nervous system is hardwired to experience the emotion that is facilitated through our sensory experiences. So if you were ever rear-ended in your car, your senses are on high alert at all times getting ready for the experience to repeat itself. You feel fear, when there is nothing out there to fear. I'll delve deeper into emotions in the next chapter.

So use your senses but really develop your intuition. You won't be sorry. Like most gifts that we tend to ignore or dismiss, intuition has something incredibly important to reveal to us. The most important truth it has to reveal is that all Life is good. Always. *No matter what.* Our lives and all our experiences are, generally speaking, appropriate for the development of our highest consciousness. This is most often the primary work I do with people who come to me for teaching and healing—helping them finally get their minds around the fact that all their Life experiences—positive and negative—were necessary, good, and entirely sent for the sole purpose of developing their consciousness.

The senses may tell us one thing and then, if we look with our intuition, we see the bigger picture. We know that everything is okay, that our lives are just as Life means them to be.

How often do you choose, on some level, to see Life as a thief that has stolen from you, that has taken something or someone from you that you once had and still want. Or do you see Life as something that is punishing you or not fulfilling a promise you believe it made to you? When you embrace this truth, you will become present with every moment of Life in a way that makes you say *Thank you. Thank you.* Developing your intuition is a key to arriving at this place.

Relatively speaking, we are all on a sliding scale of consciousness. During any given day, we might slide from relative unconsciousness to higher level awareness and consciousness based on the experiences Life brings to us for the sole purpose of developing our intuition and conscious awareness.

Intuition is not based on personal choice or feelings, and you don't need to have any particular belief, creed, or faith to develop your intuition. You can assess your own development in this area by observing your behavior, which is the truest measure of how your intuition is growing. If you come home to find your house on fire or you come home to find a thief in your house or you go to work to find someone else has been given your job or you come home to find your spouse wants a divorce, how do you respond? If you are in the grip of your senses only, they would have you believe that Life as you have known it is "over." You might scream or punch a wall or weep uncontrollably.

Your intuition, however, will immediately calm you. It will assure you that you are okay, that everything will be well. It will tell you that you have the courage and strength to get through this outer trauma because it will pass and you will have learned something so important that it will change your life forever—for the better.

You may be tempted for awhile to give in to the senses, to the outer reality of what you see, hear, touch, taste, or smell—and to the feelings that hover around your senses, especially fear, anger, guilt, and shame, which quite literally scream at you. You are used to listening to them. You've always listened to them and thought that what was happening was actually going to hurt you.

The problem with our senses is that the emotions they generate start us warring with Life. For example, say you get fired from your job. The fact is you no longer have a job. But all the emotional components are what get you going and generating disappointment, loss, fear. You worry, you fret, and then you worry some more.

Then you get another job. Whew! It worked out. You got through it. You survived. And actually, that other job wasn't that good anyway. *Now* you're okay.

But be prepared because you have created a false sense of peace that emerged because you were at war with Life, with losing your job and all that worrying and fearing you went through.

Being at war with Life can never bring true, lasting peace. War is not, and never has been, the way to everlasting peace. The peace you feel after you go to war with Life is only temporary, and it never lasts long enough to justify that stressful battle you fought with Life.

So what does Life do? It brings you another, bigger opportunity to work with loss and fear and worry, another opportunity to surrender to a different, more conscious, and more peaceful response. So maybe you lose the next job or your health or your home. Something happens that brings up those same emotional patterns as when you lost your job, and Life asks you again, *Will you go to war with me or will you be at peace with me?*

By honing your intuitive gift, you understand right away that the job you lost or whatever is happening in your life will help you heal in some way, will help someone you love in some way, will be a factor for the good in some-one's life ten hours, ten years, or ten lifetimes from now. Intuition grows in you as you overcome your habit of rely-ing on your senses and the feelings that pop up so natu-rally. Rather, intuition begs you not to get so bent out of shape by a passing circumstance that you lose your peace-ful center. It helps you stay calm so that your senses and the negative feelings they sometimes engender don't take control of you. The peace you feel is then not about surviv-ing anything. No wars were fought. This space of peace is amazing, true, and lasting.

We don't need to understand all of Life to appreciate its intense love for us. Its truest intention is to do us good and not harm. We can trust the force and order of Life to inevitably bring us what we need to grow into greater and greater consciousness and a deeper trust of Life.

Remember: we are *of* Life. We are not separate from it. By developing your intuition, you will find yourself resisting Life less and enjoying it more. And when one of us grows in conscious awareness and intuition, all of us do, for we are all *of* Life.

As you develop your intuition, it will make you aware that anything in your belief system that separates you from another person is outdated. This may come as a sur-prise. You think a person's color scares you? You think a person's sexual preference is your business? You think another's religion is so much worse than your own?

You are mistaken. You are living from your senses and the emotions they engender. Do you like being scared and judgmental? This is not a judgment, but an observation. Because when you have unwrapped your intuition and held it up to the light and used it to view Life, you will agree with me. What an opportunity you have!

Look around you. Look at yourself. Notice how people are constantly judging their experiences or the experiences of others as good or bad, fair or unfair, right or wrong. Yet not one of us has all the data or facts of the matter on which to base such judgments. Without intuition, we have no way of knowing or understanding what Life—with all its intention for good—is trying to bring about in any given situation. And we never will. So I suggest we stop declaring moments of Life right or wrong, good or bad, fair or unfair. Let's stop the war with Life.

Often we are tempted to respond to something a person says or does in a way that ensures he or she will like us, or we may intentionally behave in a way that pleases. This is another example of why honing intuition is so helpful. As we are having an inner debate about what course of action or response to make, our intuition—when it has been honed from use—will ask THE question that can decide our course: *What is the highest good in this situation for the greatest number of people?*

You see, the point of Life is to learn how to have the best relationship possible with a force beyond our comprehension. And we do that not by reducing Life to our ignorant judgments as if Life is trying to harm us or by analyzing it to death. Rather, when you learn to navigate Life intuitively, you can count on your intuition to guide you to do what is in the highest good in every situation and ask Life's foremost question because Life intends only the highest good.

We do not have to settle for faith or hope. There is something more. Your intuition knows Life is okay *no matter what*. It is okay not just right now or today but in the past and in the future. Always. If you align your intention with the highest good, you align with Life itself. Intuition is the key.

How do you get to that platform where any Life experience becomes okay, all the time? It takes patience and practice, an open heart, and the willingness to use your intuition. It's a process of awakening consciousness. And then that possibility of Life in all its manifestations being okay leads to the probability of everything being okay. That probability of being okay eventually becomes an absolute okay.

Enter Life's classroom if you like and become its student and you will see. Or, save yourself some suffering and open to these truths. Many people think that healing happens because you *understand* what happened in your life. That's the old mentality. Let's just be healed. Let's allow Life—all of it—to be okay. Always.

∾ 3. ∾
THE TRUTH
ABOUT FEELINGS

I AM ONE WHO hugs and enjoys being held. I am one who loves and enjoys being loved. I am one who experiences and enjoys being experienced. I am one who lives and embraces death.

In this lesson, I go deeper into the truth about feelings or emotions. This chapter may make you vibrate with understanding and a sense of relief and meaning. Or, you may find yourself strongly resisting—even rejecting—these truths. Embrace whatever you may feel about this lesson because it's not something spoken of openly.

The truth is this: **You will come to realize and accept that at a certain point in the evolution of your consciousness, you will no longer need feelings to define yourself.**

In their truest sense, feelings are nothing but conditioned reactions based on our perception of any given moment. Most feelings, if not all, are based on past experiences, and our feelings about them. Or, we make a hypothesis about a potential future experience that hasn't happened, based on our feeling about a past or present circumstance. So we may feel worried, fearful, or happy about something that has not yet happened because of a past experience.

We've been conditioned to believe that we *are* what we feel. Perceptually, it may be true that we are our feelings. Studies show that emotions play a role in dictating molecular motion inside the body. Literally, emotions dictate chemistry to some degree and that chemistry, in one form or another, plays a large role in what we are.

The truth is: You are not your feelings. You do not need feelings to have an unconditionally loving relationship with Life.

Believe me when I tell you that there will come a time when you will go forward into a higher space of consciousness in which you will no longer need to see your feelings as the truth of what you are; you will no longer need your feelings. In this higher space of consciousness, you will see feelings for what they really are: *reactions to Life.* Then you can embrace feelings for what they were to you when you were in a past space of consciousness. Never reject the stages of your inner spiritual development. All the stages of consciousness are perfect; we need to go through them all.

Going forward, accept the possibility—no, the inevitability—of a relationship with Life that does not contain many feelings, an existence that is not controlled by your feelings. This is a major evolutionary space for every soul on the planet. You will evolve past a point of needing feelings to guide you.

My purpose here is to make you aware of this truth and to bring a level of awareness to the subject of feelings. In no way, shape, or form am I suggesting that you suppress any feeling. We do not reach a place of intuitive peace by suppressing feelings or emotions. As I said, we need to experience feelings because we are students in Life's classroom. We can go through as many feelings as we need to, and believe as many times as we have to, that we *are* those feelings until we become more aware and understand the truth.

In the meantime, you don't have to accept your own feelings or another's feelings as the ultimate truth of who you are, or of what Life is. Accept that you have had billions of emotional experiences through an infinite number of lifetimes. All of these feelings have had an effect on your emotional interpretation of what you consider to be "real." As you accept deeper truths, you will understand that what you have felt to be "real" and "true"—based on your feelings—may, in fact, *not be*.

Just to be clear, I'm not suggesting that you reject the feelings you have or the emotions you express. Rather, begin to make a shift into a space where you no longer rely on your highly subjective, erratic, and instinctual emotions. After all, an emotional response to a moment—and Life is an eternal string of moments—is unsustainable. Instead, embrace a higher level of intuitive consciousness and guidance, which is based in the truth that all

Life is good. Only through using intuition, through growing into a higher level of intuitive consciousness, will we have a sustainable ongoing relationship to Life in a space of unconditional love, acceptance, and peace.

As a student in Life's classroom, I became interested in feelings when people began coming to me with feelings they could not trace back to a source. They could not consciously justify why they had *these feelings*. Their life was good, they told me, yet, they had these feelings, these strongly triggered feelings. I began to question the validity of these emotions they could not explain. I was able, in my space of consciousness, to open up to the unconscious or subconscious minds of my patients. This is where feelings are stored—feelings we either could not handle, blocked out, or were unaware of. But because feelings need to be released, those people's feelings, which they couldn't explain, were being triggered out of them. This is how I became aware that a person's feelings are not always based on what is going on *now*. I came to understand that feelings are often inaccurate; therefore, they are probably not accurate guides for our lives in the now.

Past-life experiences are considered questionable by many people. But let me tell you what I've learned about them. You may or may not accept past-life experiences as real, but past-life experiences have also played a role in my patients' emotional reactions. Some patients have looked to me for guidance and I have seen mental, emotional, physical, and spiritual symptoms diminish if not resolve when past-life emotional patterns are released. My patients were completely unaware of these patterns, and these patterns were not the reason they came to see me. My patients taught me so much about Life and about emotions. They were my teachers in disguise.

It's not necessary to accept the reality of past lives to follow and accept the teachings in *The Practice*. No one has been more of a skeptic than I about this. As I teach this truth, I run the risk of looking the fool more than anyone. As Life taught me these truths, they became real—and undeniable. Whether you believe this truth or not is irrelevant. I too once lived in a limited space. We all do.

Eventually, you will see the eternity that is Life. If this truth does not resonate with you now, it will at some appropriate time. Be patient until that time comes—because it certainly will. You do not need to "believe" to accept the teachings in *The Practice*. If you came to this book with an open heart and a mind willing to change, then try to become aware of feelings you experience but cannot explain to yourself. Engage a deeper level of awareness that is always available to you when you have a feeling or express an emotion that confuses you, that you cannot identify as being appropriate to your present situation. It may be a feeling that goes all the way back to your birth—or *in utero* for we receive our mother's emotions and feelings—and that feeling only needs to be acknowledged, accepted, and released. If you find yourself mired in emotions that you can't explain, if you want to be released from all of your life's emotional patterns, enter into your past life without judgment.

Be aware that if you begin a genuine release of past-life trauma, you will not always find that you were a king, a queen, or a princess. Anyone who's done past-life release with me knows that we don't often find those rarefied conditions. So we must be open beyond what we are conscious of if we truly want to be released from emotional patterns and from working our way through Life by our feelings. Enter into the space of past life in the same way you enter into all other spaces of Life, without judgment. Judging the past, present, or future will never bring us the healing we need. Releasing it will!

Let's get really honest about our feelings. If you accept that you are growing in intuitive consciousness—or you are already in the space of intuitive consciousness—then there is no reason not to be completely honest. So I'm going to ask you to reflect on the majority of your lifetime emotional experiences. Don't judge them but look at all of them objectively for a moment. Would you put the majority of your feelings you remember most clearly in the "feel good" or the "feel bad" category?

In the end, there is no real "bad." We've already discussed that truth. But our feelings experience Life at a level of consciousness where "good" and "bad" still exist. Even though we're all heading toward a place of intuitive knowing where everything is all good, you may still, to various degrees, rely on feelings. So, from that perspective, into which category would you put most of your feelings—good or bad?

I've seen an amazing cross-section of humanity over the past fifteen years, and most people tell me that they most often remember the "bad" or negative feelings, so that would be where they put the majority of their most easily recalled emotional experiences.

Why would that be the case? Why do we remember or recall more "bad" feelings than "good" feelings?

There may be lots of good feelings, but, in general, the first function of feelings is to keep us alive, which means they are based on a finite relationship with short-term experiences. Those "bad" feelings are primitive reaction patterns that are meant to defend us and keep us out of harm's way. They keep us from dangerous and unpleasant experiences. To defend us, do they make us feel safe and comfortable? No! They make us feel uncomfortable—and they do an amazing job of it. If they make us feel uncomfortable again and again and again, why do we continue to rely on them?

We rely on emotions to keep us safe. Yet the basis of being kept safe and out of harm's way is really based on a short-term, finite relationship with all Life experiences. Feelings and emotions create only a false sense of safety. They function on some level as an avoidance system. They never get us to a space of an eternal relationship with Life based on unconditional love, acceptance, and peace so that we no longer have to avoid Life experiences.

Feelings create pylons, a veritable obstacle course that keeps us living small and not free. A pylon is an experience in Life that we have judged as negative through perceptual data. We are not in harmony with the experience. We feel "bad." So the next time we experience a similar situation, we put up a pylon so that we don't feel as "bad." I liken it to walking into a room where a bucket of water falls on your head. You don't like it. But you walk into another room and another bucket of water falls on your head. So you put up a pylon so that you don't have to walk into any more rooms so that no more buckets of water fall on you. The space in which you now live gets smaller and smaller with all those pylons you've set up to avoid feeling bad. Life now becomes an obstacle course. Even if sometimes you slip past a pylon, you breathe a sigh of relief, *Whew! I made it past the pylon! The water didn't get me that time!*

But are you free to really live? No! There are too many pylons, and you are always afraid. But even living small like this is a blessing in disguise because once you recognize that you are erecting pylons all over the place, that awareness forces you to begin to release the emotions that set up those pylons.

Of course, there never were actual pylons, were there? They were only emotions based on some past experience that made you fearful. You can let it go, die to it, in a sense. I think it's a good idea to die every day to emotions that no longer serve us.

If you still need pylons, put them up. It's okay if you don't want to experience what's in any "room" of Life, so to speak. If you do set up a pylon so you don't have to enter some "room" or situation in Life, then you don't yet realize that you can always choose to enter the room from a place of unconditional love and peace.

Are you beginning to see that the energy behind

the pylons—the reason they appear—is your emotions or feelings about a certain moment or experience that is based on either a past experience or a future experience that hasn't even happened? All these emotional experiences are based on judgments. The emotional experience creates ignorant judgments of "good" or "bad" and those judgments become the truth. But they are not truth, they are only judgments based on reactions.

As I said, you will eventually no longer need to make your life smaller by erecting pylons. The "bad" feelings that created them will effortlessly disappear—for those feelings are woefully inadequate guides for living Life in the present moment. They will disappear as you grow in consciousness.

Take a moment to process this teaching and to observe your emotions as you read this. You don't have to have faith in me about this, or faith that I'm telling you the truth. If what I'm saying doesn't resonate with you as truth, okay; become a student of Life and find out for yourself. You will go through more suffering, but you still come to the same truth. All I ask is that you open up to what I'm saying, hear it, and consider that there's a certain degree of merit in what I'm saying:

- Most easily recalled feelings are or have been, for the majority of us, a negative or "bad" experience;
- A major function of feelings is to keep us out of harm's way or keep us from getting hurt emotionally, spiritually, physically;
- Feelings do have a function, and in their proper place, they can be useful—

Big things in Life sneak up on us sometimes, but most of the time the big things are nothing but the big gorilla in the room, and we've been living Life and getting around the big gorilla for some time. What I like to do is confront the gorilla and allow the release of feelings to happen. If you try this, you will find, like I did, that you will become very centered and peaceful no matter what the gorilla looks like, no matter what the situation. I'm no longer very emotional about any situation because I've already released all my emotions. So what's left?

There's nothing to do but be with any situation that arises just as it is, peacefully. Besides, the end point is not about releasing feelings. The end point is about loving Life. Isn't that wonderful!

Are there good feelings? Yes. Good feelings are almost always based on situations in which we feel completely comfortable and safe. Good feelings can be a constant presence in our lives, as I've already said when we let our intuition guide us. Intuition is the best foundation for having good feelings. Why? Because when you live based on the truth that all Life is good, then the feelings you have are most often based in that goodness.

I like to say "have intuition for dinner and feelings for dessert." Nice feelings are sweet. They really are: holding a baby, kissing a loved one, hugging or being held. They're sweet, but let's face it, they are not the majority of moments.

We need to be realistic about how we experience the eternity that is Life. Most people live for those sweet moments—and merely "survive" everything else. Yet, they eventually wonder why they feel sad, disappointed, or unhappy most of the time.

Now do you see? When we live purely from our emotions, we have to know that the sweet moments are mathematically miniscule compared to other experiences that don't generate that sweetness. Still, we keep living for the sweet moments because that's what we've always done. We still don't get that there is another possibility: That *all* moments are perfect.

The positive side of feelings

Feeling "great"—that sweet moment—can be just as out of balance as feeling "bad." That moment of feeling euphoric or emotionally great is the beginning of all addiction. This brings me to another truth. **All addiction is rooted in feeling euphoric in an unsustainable manner for unsustainable reasons.**

If that isn't a truth that sets you free, then you're just not ready to be set free. Addiction is seated in that euphoric moment when you feel completely free from most or all of your negative feelings and pain. And more powerful than that, not only does that feeling become addictive, but so does the entire situation, whatever it may be. We literally photograph it energetically and store it in our being. So everyone, and every substance, and everything in that situation becomes an integral part of what we need to re-experience that euphoria.

So if you're euphoric and you're having a drink, alcohol becomes a part of the experience that needs to be replicated; if you are euphoric and the sun's out, the sun becomes a part of the addiction; if you're euphoric and you're having an orgasm, that becomes a part of the addiction. If you are with one or more persons and you experience euphoria, then that person or persons become a requirement for the experience to repeat itself. The emotional addiction is then embraced and interconnected with a substance, person, setting. In that space, you are then addicted to both the feeling and the experience that supports it or allows it to be. That is a powerful truth.

The end of addiction is to live intuitively. *Being* is what we are when we develop our intuition. *Being* means we are *with* Life, not reacting to Life, but being with Life. We are *being*—not doing, not achieving, not even becoming.

When we live this way we can be present with Life and be at peace. So you too will be one who hugs and enjoys being held. You too will be one who loves and enjoys being loved. You too will be one who experiences and enjoys being experienced. You will live and embrace death. You will be able to do so from a space of higher consciousness.

That doesn't mean we need to be isolated, alone, or insulated from Life. We don't need to be inert to be at peace. We can interact with anyone at any time, in any situation, at any energetic frequency and maintain our inner space of *being*, our peace.

Otherwise, what is the point of living? If all I needed to be at peace was to be alone, I would have been done years ago. But I found these truths incredibly helpful in my own life and very freeing that I wanted to bring these teachings forth so that everyone can be in a space where we can maintain a state of conscious peace, love, acceptance, and compassion—with everyone else.

As you go forward, you will begin to see this lesson everywhere you look. You'll begin to realize how many things are done and how many decisions are made based on emotions and feelings—and the result. When we are awake and aware of feelings and their effect on our lives, we begin to understand that feelings are not stable and predictable guides. They cannot be the foundation for a sustainable, eternally peaceful experience. We've expected them to give us peace but they haven't. But that is not their purpose. Instead they've led us into addictions of all kinds.

Releasing feelings and moving into intuition is the transition for those who are ready. Maybe you—or someone you know—isn't even aware of intuition. Yet, by hearing this teaching, they become conscious of the fact that there is something beyond feelings, something beyond using perceptual data as a way to live.

In closing, be conscious of how you use your feelings and to what level you are letting them dictate your path in Life. Don't criticize them or judge them. Don't be hard on yourself when you find them running your life again. We are all at a point somewhere between the unknown beginning and an infinite end. It doesn't matter where you are on the path. Wherever you are, then that's where you are. The force of Life will move all of us from the space of relative unconsciousness into a space of higher relative consciousness.

When the moment is appropriate, these steps in *The Practice* will resonate within you as truth. You will be ready for the next step. Be patient until that moment comes.

✨ 4. ✨
LETTING GO
OF FEELINGS

DID YOU KNOW that you don't have to have feelings? Did you realize you have the option to *not* have an emotion? You can stop hitting yourself with that emotional hammer. Not having feelings is a really legitimate way to live.

The transition from an emotionally reactive guidance system into intuitive knowing is a natural transition, though not an absolute segue. Again, you must embrace your emotions as long as is necessary in as balanced a way as possible, allowing as many experiences as Life deems necessary to bring you to this transition—a transition that is eventually inevitable. You'll get there, but don't "work" at it. It's not about working hard to get there. It's not even about trying to "get past" your feelings. Don't force yourself or force anyone else.

As you proceed and move into a space of unconditional love and acceptance, you will inevitably and effortlessly let go of feelings as the definition of who and what you are. Become aware, accept, and allow this peaceful transition from relying on emotions and feelings to moving into intuitive knowing. It will come peacefully, effortlessly, naturally. We are all on an individual spiritual journey—together.

For these reasons and others to be discussed, as we all make this transition from relying on feelings to engaging and living from our intuition, don't stop trying to have emotions, but simply become aware of the possibility of experiencing Life without them. Then realize that you are going to release many stored emotions. These are not new emotions but are those that have been stored in your body, mind, and spirit—emotions that need to be released. These emotions may be past memories that are now being released by your higher consciousness in an orderly fashion and in the highest good.

Emotions will still come up but you will not be generating many new emotions—and not for much longer. Just be aware, accept, and release stored, old, suppressed emotions that simply need to come out. These are the primary feelings that are stored in us, that we use to habitually respond to current situations even though they are based on past experiences—and even past-life experiences. Avoid judging them for they cannot be judged. Just release them.

A small part of you will continue to generate new emotions as you move into a space of greater consciousness, but it will be an insignificant amount, and they will continue to diminish as you move forward. As you go through this transition, some of your beliefs may be challenged.

Everyone who has come to see me has done emotional release as a part of his or her visits. We find that situations and emotions are tied into certain parts of the body. They affect the body and contribute to symptoms of disease. That's when we do an emotional release. Sometimes, people ask me to tell them what emotion they're releasing, but sometimes I don't know. If I do know, I only tell them what emotion they are releasing if it's in the highest good for them to know; otherwise it's irrelevant. The beautiful part is that most people who come to see me have moved into a space in which they no longer care what emotion is being released. They just want the emotion gone. They've been doing *The Practice* and they know their intuition – without emotions—is a much better guide.

Emotions are reactions to reality based on past programming; they arise as a result of a reaction to reality. It becomes a personal choice to follow these old reactions. We follow them when we mistakenly think we can rely on them to guide us. *I'm upset with what Sally did to me so I'm not going to Sally's birthday party.* Or, *I'm angry with you so I'm not going to get along with you.*

Yet, in many ways, feelings are simply primitive reactions to Life. We can rely on them until we realize they are not the most credible and honest way to guide our lives. The emotion is unbidden but the reaction is where the personal choice comes in. Instead of immediately choosing to follow those emotions, stop, reflect, and consult your intuition. Allow your intuition to choose your response, rather than your primitive emotional reaction.

I suffered so much when I chose to go with feelings that I had to eventually give feelings up for good. How many times do I need to hit myself in the hand with a hammer before "hitting myself with a hammer" is no longer a "choice?" When I know that I'm going to hurt my hand, I stop hitting myself—that's when.

I was surprised when I learned this truth. I surrendered and began letting feelings go. I tried this out before I ever passed it on to my patients or before I wrote about it. As I moved into this space of releasing feelings and emotions, of course that's when Life challenged me most. That's the amazing thing about Life—it gives you what you need to grow in consciousness.

So that was exactly when my marriage became emotionally challenging, when my wife and I began to have children, and when I bought, renovated, and moved into a new building that God had given me in a vision years earlier. God, through Life, gave me so much at once because those were the challenging times in my life when I'd fall back on feelings. I'd feel overwhelmed. *There is just too much going on! I can't handle this. How could she do this to me? Doesn't she know how hard I'm working?*

Feelings, feelings, feelings! I had so many feelings, and sure, they were genuine, but were they good for me? Were they the best guides to my highest good and the highest good of my family? No! I just kept hitting myself with them. So this was an important time for me. Life brought me what I needed to put the hammer down—for good.

I don't have many feelings now, but when I get into a

situation that triggers a feeling, I invite the situation and feeling into awareness. I'm open because I know something I no longer need is being released. Life is cleaning me of something. When it happens to you, you will know it is the truth.

When Life presents the possibility that you might not have your house in a month, and you reply, "Okay, I'll be fine." And when you might not have your job in three months, and you reply, "Okay, I'll be fine."—that's when you know you're deep into *The Practice.*

So how do we release emotions? How do we surrender them? First, become aware again that feelings are not necessarily the best guidance system for living and acknowledge that at some point you won't need them. At some point, you will enter a state of being where you will not have the highs and lows, the ups and down of emotions; at some point, emotions will, believe it or not, cease to exist to a large extent.

Second, become conscious of what feelings do to you, especially when you don't always know why you feel a certain way. Become aware of their source. You really don't need to understand your feelings any more than this. You need to get the unnecessary feelings out of the way because they are no longer in your highest good. People are at different stages in this matter. Most people are aware of their feelings, and have worked with them to some degree. A few people have really done too much work on them and just need to let them go. And, there are some people who need to begin to experience their feelings first before moving on to releasing them. Yet, this teaching is applicable to your life no matter where you are in the process of growing more conscious.

Third, as *The Practice* teaches, embrace your feelings with the proper perspective. Love your feelings whatever they are and wherever they come from, but with the ultimate goal of moving beyond them to a place not of feeling but of simply being. If you need to work on feelings to resolve and release them, then do so. But, if you follow *The Practice*, feelings will, at some point, cease, naturally, inevitably.

As you release emotion, as you embrace intuition, as you follow *The Practice*, you will be naturally released from addiction as a byproduct of *The Practice* itself. You will be released from your quest for that "sweet" moment and that "good" feeling as well as from your need to avoid those "bad" feelings.

What will take the place of feelings, good and bad, sweet and painful? You will find a peaceful bliss in just being with Life. And you can do this for all eternity. It is a sustainable alternative to relying on feelings. You will need no other external substance, environment, or person to achieve this state of peaceful bliss, which is not a feeling but a state of being. As you grow into your intuition, as you rely on your inner intuitive truth to translate and interpret your external environment, you will find this peace. At some point, your inner reality will remain peaceful and unconditionally loving no matter what your outer experiences may be. *The Practice* gives you a stable inner foundation—a place of *being*—from which to interact with Life.

These teachings also eliminate any need we may feel to protect ourselves from what some people call the "darker" energies, or evil, as it's been known for ages. I find such references quite hilarious. I used to protect myself from these energies—because I once feared them. But as I developed my intuition, released feelings, and moved into a state of being, I now see everything as God, and all of it as good. It was always all God and all good—but I just didn't know it yet, back then.

So these darker energies that we fear, that we try to protect ourselves from, are lesser-evolved fields of God. Remember each of us is a field of God/Life and we are all a field of God and so is everything else. So what are we protecting ourselves from? Do you see?

If you want to—if this is your time to—live sustainably in a space of unconditional love and peace, then you have no choice but to live intuitively and to *be* with Life. If you are not conscious of the intuitive power in your life, if it is not a reality for you in any way, if it hasn't been awakened to any significant level then, of course, emotions and feelings are appropriate and beneficial as a guidance system because they keep you safe, they keep you going forward—you learn, you grow.

If and when it is your turn to evolve, you will at least know where you're going—to a space of peaceful bliss—and you won't be afraid of the unknown. Eventually, every one of us will arrive in an intuitive space of consciousness. It is the end of the story—and the beginning—all at the same time.

SPEAKING
THE TRUTH

IN THIS CHAPTER, I want to focus on how our history with feelings affects our ability to speak the truth or follow the truth as we know it. Are you aware of how, for example, your feelings or potential emotional reactions inhibit you from being completely honest? How many times have you *not* said something truthful because you didn't want to hurt another person's feelings? Many times there's an emotional reason not to be honest. So we have to wonder, How much of what we're doing with other people is authentic?

If we can look at ourselves objectively, we'll find this behavior pattern in our repertoire, and we'll notice that we overuse it much of the time. As a result, we find ourselves in a compromised state outside of our highest good.

We value the *potential* emotional reaction of another person more than we value our deepest truth, a truth that will—if we honor it—bring us into greater alignment with the eternal truths of Life, one of which we've already mentioned: All Life is good, no matter what.

Yet, we continue to put another person's emotional approval ahead of our purpose, which is allowing yourself to come into divine order with Life, and, therefore, with God. We bow to and give allegiance to a subjective reaction instead of an objective intuitive truth.

It's critical that harmony with the order of Life comes first. Harmony means we tell the truth. We must primarily obligate ourselves to our relationship with Life. We must put Life first because we have an *eternal* relationship with Life.

Instead, we continually react to what others *might* think, say, or do by becoming dishonest. Our dishonesty creates a false sense of fragile peace that we hope will last at least a moment longer, and we cling to the hope that nothing will disturb that fragile peace. But peace based on lies will not last. Yet we lie anyway. Eventually, despite our dishonest attempts at peace, the relationship and the fragile peace spiral into dysfunction. Then we begin to fear and dread a relationship's ending—even if there are no signs of it ending—because that's what has always happened. We remember the pattern.

Inevitably, the best thing is to tell the truth and let what's going to happen *happen*; allow a true resolution to be reached. Then you'll be in harmony with Life, though it might not *feel* like it.

This may sound a bit dramatic, but it is not overstated, I assure you. I see people gambling with their peace every day because of their addiction to external approval—and their willingness to bet on it again and again.

We are here to tell each other the truth, from our deepest space of knowing, and to practice living Life in a way that unveils that truth so we can share it with others. Someone may disagree with you and react to what you say, but, if you're deepest intention is to connect to the intuitive truth within you and to be unconditionally loving, accepting, and compassionate to all beings, then you need fear nothing. With this intention, you *can* be truthful to the best of your ability, for yourself and for others. Believe me, people are not only looking for the truth, they are also looking to be healed by it. By telling the truth, you validate another's truth. In turn, you allow them to share truth with others, multiplying the overall effect of truth within the field of Life. This is Life's deepest intention.

At times there is no way to tell the truth without hurting someone's feelings. When we don't tell the truth just to save someone from an unpleasant feeling, not only do we lose our relationship with Life but we also lose our integrity with the person we are dealing with because they see us as an enabler of their own dishonesty. When we don't tell others the truth, we impede their highest good and we lose our connection with Life itself, which counts on our integrity.

Life doesn't lie to us. It is always telling us the truth, so why wouldn't the truth be the point at which we all start—and stay? If we are able to see the truth in Life, why wouldn't we say it to another person?

One example is death, where there's an expectation of grieving and sadness. In such an emotionally vulnerable situation, it is very difficult to tell the truth. Why? Because people are emotionally distraught, and there is an unconscious pattern in all of us that if someone is already emotionally upset, we don't want to say anything that's going to make it worse.

I love that—"make it worse."

We assume that the emotional space that person is in is bad because they're experiencing this situation, and they're feeling grief. So now we've labeled that emotional experience as "bad" and the result as "grief." Now there is tension because people will think there is something wrong with you if you are not sad and not grieving. This is a perfect example of a situation in which we are too afraid to speak the truth as we know it. Even if you know that it was a long, drawn out death that zapped the family of energy and strength, you still tell them, "I'm so sorry for your loss," instead of the more honest and truthful, "I'm glad his suffering and your suffering is over." You aren't honest because you don't want to make it "worse" than it already is.

The next time you're at a funeral, reflect on the truth of the situation. Rather than automatically saying something innocuous that won't upset anyone, tell the truth as you know it. *Thank God he finally passed. His illness was putting such an emotional and physical strain on the family, and his quality of life was never going to return. I am happy for everyone involved.*

I am one who loves death. I see it as a part of Life, as a birth to the other side. It's a transition point into a future Life in another form. If I'm stuck being obedient to emotions that are proscribed, I'll never allow myself to know and be that truth without feeling bad that I know it.

Let's stay committed to the reality of Life, which is that we will experience death an infinite number of times. You may feel an immediate resistance to that truth because we all have a level of ignorance that allows us to believe we still have a choice where death is concerned. But the statement is true. Become a student of Life and find this truth for yourself.

Life doesn't lie about death because death is an inevitable part of the cycle. When we lose our integrity by defaulting into a habituated emotional response about death without giving real reflection to the truth, we enable that person to continue to deny that death is <u>not</u> part of the cycle of Life, as if it is something altogether awful that has happened to a certain individual. By not telling the truth, we set people up for more suffering in the future.

Of course, a person's emotional response is never wrong because it is always based on his or her current level of consciousness. Yet if we don't speak the truth from a loving peaceful place, while respecting a person's emotional state—and telling the truth—we don't do them any service. There is always room for a drop of truth, a word, a phrase.

In one sense we tell people the truth when we say, "He is in a better place, his suffering is over." But we are so cautious about how we say it! We don't want to say the wrong thing.

The compassionate thing to do when you are at a wake or talking to someone who has lost a loved one to death is to remember what it was like when you were deeply affected by death and how you were governed by your emotions. Have compassion for where people are, but, at the same time, don't fear telling the truth. Compassion and honesty do not conflict. You are not judging their situation; you are telling them the truth.

"I can understand how much you must miss him. I can understand what a shock this is. He was only thirty years old. It must be so hard to understand how these things happen. These moments in Life are so far beyond our comprehension. We'll never understand why these things happen. We'll never make a whole lot of sense of this because we don't really understand the eternity of Life."

Each of the things I just said—and I have said to people— are compassionate but full of truth and honesty. With this kind of honesty, we can release a mother, father, son, or daughter from trying to *understand* why a loved one has moved on. We release the grieving person from blaming Life, from creating a conflict between herself or himself and Life. And the truth is: We will never know why! Through such a compassionate and truthful way of speaking, you can release a person from some, if not all of that suffering.

We hang onto emotions out of habit. You may still feel grief and loss if you still believe something has happened to you or to someone you love. Yet, you can still learn about Life from the emotional processes of grief and loss, for example. It's true that such emotions have a purpose: they help us evolve to a higher level of consciousness. A particular situation, such as death, was created for the evolution of all, for the evolution of consciousness. So although such emotions will continue, they are a response to a part of Life that has happened. As I've said, you will still choose to rely on emotions—until you don't.

Once we are done with experiencing Life with our emotions, we will still see emotions in others. But, remember, there are an infinite number of experiences before our consciousness can grow into a place of peace with Life and peace with the necessary part death plays. Then the choice around relying on emotions no longer exists. If you haven't reached that place of peace with Life and death, allow yourself to view grief as beautiful—until you know the truth about emotions—and reach that space of peace!

Grief is not going anywhere, just like death, so it doesn't have to be a part of your experience in the same way it has been in the past. And grief doesn't have to stop you from being truthful.

I've given you an intuitive interpretation of the emotional expressions of grief and loss. Doesn't the intuitive way make a lot more sense than judging the expression of an emotion and then compromising your truth by saying and doing what you've always said and done because you fear the judgment of others?

You can always continue to learn the hard way, if you

must—but if you speak your truth from a place of love and compassion, no matter what others may think, say, or do, you will come to love and accept the truth. You will come to peace with death and loss and grief in such a way that you can share that peace with everyone you meet.

By speaking the truth we are also telling someone who is grieving a death this: *You are still in the field of Life. There are people around you who love you. It is in the highest good to experience this death, move through it, and get back to Life, to loving people and to the things that bring you joy.*When you speak this way, you are releasing the person from trying to figure it out, from feeling that she has to respond emotionally in a habituated way.

My grandmother passed in her sleep, but before she died she said, "On the day that I die, the birds will still be singing, the sun will be shining, and Life will be continuing on." Her death was completely non-eventful. Life will go on. That is consciousness. That is someone who is not denying anything.

You can apply these basic principles (that I've applied to death and loss) to any situation. Here's another: *I know it is difficult to appreciate why your husband left you. Relationships are always changing forms. I know it is difficult to understand why these things happen. There is not a lot of sense to this, and we don't understand. We must accept when relationships change form, release the emotions, and get back into a loving relationship with Life. We just don't know.*

By being compassionate *and* truthful, you're not enabling someone to become emotionally stagnant. You are inducing them to move forward, which we all know in our heart is something we need to do. Yet we often become afraid of being and living our truth: *What will people think if I'm not heartbroken, if I move forward too soon?*

No matter what space we are in, no matter what situation, Life is not going to stop. Life will keep moving on. This is the reality. Life will go on and on and on. We need to practice with each experience, we need to be the student and learn. So Practice.

Again, if we don't know the freedom of telling the truth about Life, we get into hoping that we say the right thing, which is usually *not* the truthful thing. We know dishonesty usually doesn't work, but we gamble on it over and over again.

You cannot be truth and speak truth with any consistency if you are going to decide the question based on your own or another's feelings. Get past the inevitability of feelings, come to peace with the fact that you and others will continue to have feelings, and decide, despite feelings, to be intuitively connected with the truth.

Will others like you for being truth and speaking truth? You may not always be embraced and supported by those around you. People will expect you to exhibit specific feelings in certain situations. As you move into this higher space of intuition, and you are no longer as reactive, you are going to confront some unusual reactions from other people. The choice is between an emotional response and the responsibility to be honest based on intuitive knowing. Be and live and speak truth anyway.

Experiences like death and loss will never stop happening. We tend to believe that death and the emotions
surrounding it will happen a limited number of times.
The emotions are so painful that we don't want them to
happen again. Yet, every experience will happen an infinite number of times, either to us or to someone we know.

In reality, we are all one, and if something happens to
you, it happens to me, and it happens to everyone. This is
the truth of every possible experience. All possible experiences will continue to happen—and they happen to all
of us because we are all one. Each experience will be an
infinite presence, forever.

Finally, you get it. It's not all about you. It's all about Life.

When you get this truth, when you see someone going
through a necessary emotional experience, you don't
withdraw the truth from that person, because you don't
see them going through a "bad" or "hurtful" emotional
experience—because you know the truth that there are no
bad emotional experiences.

Therefore, you don't have to fix them, you don't have
that burden of needing to help them or feel you have to
make the situation better. The situation is fine and appropriate for their current space of consciousness, whatever it
is. Their experience is necessary in ways you may or may
not understand. So you are no longer judging them in their
moment of emotional expression. Instead, intuitively, you
are embracing and unconditionally loving that particular
moment of Life as it presents itself either directly or indirectly in your life. You see it as a beautiful step toward

higher consciousness. You are there with the experience and you learn from it, surrendering into it from as great a space of love and peace as you can.

∽ 6. ∾
STAYING
IN BALANCE

I HOPE I'VE HELPED you better understand the effect of emotions on the way you experience all of Life. Perhaps I've initiated a shift, or extended a shift you've already begun, to living from a more intuitive approach.

I want to delve deeper into the energy needed to live emotionally, to explain how it affects our bodies, and to define why living this way is not efficient or sustainable.

First, if you look back in history, the evidence of our emotional and unsustainable behaviors is littered throughout. There was balance in creation when humanity lived in harmony with all other creatures, when humans understood they were no better than any other species, that they would both be consumed and consume. Mutual respect for the needs of all made it possible for all beings to live in balance.

Other, earlier cultures—Mayan, Incan, American Indian—lived from their intuition, respecting the order of Life, enabling humans and other life forms to live in balance, which benefited both nature and humans. Indigenous cultures today have withstood the test of time because they have not created imbalance on the planet.

History has demonstrated how empires or world powers rise and how they fall, how they succeed and how they fail. Every time they conquer, they find a need to conquer more; eventually, what is conquered has to be sustained by the conquerors. Talk about imbalance! Imbalance in a culture almost always precedes collapse. Empires fail, then balance is restored, at least for a time.

When we live emotionally—as individuals or humanity as a whole—we live independently without awareness of the other, in a kind of empire of self, which is costly to maintain, not only for ourselves but for the rest of Life as well. Everything is affected by the choices we make based on our emotional fluctuations—and the resulting material circumstances that we think we need for Life to be okay. Left to our own emotional guidance system, we'll be led to create an unsustainable reality—an emotional empire that will eventually collapse again and again and again. As we continue to build an egocentric creation that is even bigger and even better, it is inevitable that what we build will collapse. We blame ourselves for the failure, tell ourselves that we aren't good enough yet, or what we built wasn't good enough, or blame Life for the collapse and mutter about how unfair Life is or how unlucky we are.

These are lies we tell ourselves. Yet, what do we do? We start again, imagining a different outcome as we rebuild an even bigger and better unsustainable reality that will eventually collapse again. It's a never-ending cycle. We call ourselves "caretakers" of the planet, but, in truth, we cannot take care of ourselves in a way that does not destroy the Life around us and in us.

I would venture to say that the reason humanity has a global, unsustainable energy issue is because, as individuals, we each initially developed an inefficient and unsustainable energy issue within our own lives due to our emotional responses to our environment, each other, and our experiences. We keep thinking we *have* to respond emotionally—and we do so at any cost—to maintain what we think we need. We never take the time to honestly evaluate if all our emotional energy is necessary, sustainable, and in the highest good.

It wasn't until humanity became consumers, generally speaking, that we began to see ourselves egotistically as better than other Life forms and worthy of more of the resources. We looked at nature in terms of *What can it do for us? What can we take?* Humanity quickly became emotionally attached to having more, taking more, and being more. We ceased living for the greatest good of all. This kind of relationship with Life is—and will continue to be—unsustainable if we continue to believe that we are the most important living creatures on earth.

As we look to be more sustainable and efficient as a society, it makes sense that the most important place to begin is with our own lives, individually, not only in terms of the car we drive, the house we live in, or whether we recycle, but in terms of every facet of our lives. If our journey is to be truly sustainable throughout eternity, we must start within.

How then do we begin to live fully, which is the purpose of Life, which is *The Practice*? If Life is primarily based on meeting our own needs to the exclusion of others' needs, how can Life —which intends only good—fulfill its best intention for us? When we live with a culture of imbalance, Life—or nature—will outlast us in any fight we wish to have with it. This is an important truth.

Imbalance inevitably occurs because of the following truth: **The emotional experience of Life is subjective, and is governed by emotional reactions that fluctuate based on individual or collective interpretations of Life. These reactions are very energy intensive.**

Contrast this truth with another: **The intuitive experience of Life is objective and is based on being with all of Life from a space of love, acceptance, and peace. It does not require emotional fluctuations. This experience is more aligned with the highest good for all forms of Life. It is much less energy intensive.**

At some point, enough unconsciousness will transform into consciousness and intuition will replace emotion, and we will surrender the dream of independence, come to peace, and begin *The Practice*. We will put ourselves into Life's classroom and become its student, dedicating our lives to the highest good of all.

Only then will we understand that we didn't *really* need bigger and better, we didn't really benefit by an egocentric creation, by being so independent. We finally see that our emotional fluctuations never served us or others.

What we need to do, we learn, is to completely surrender to Life—absent of any self-interest—so that we can live in harmony with all of Life. It's that simple.

When we live emotionally, which is evident in how we interact as a society on so many levels, we approach Life from an unsustainable place. Life will bring us back into balance –as it always has, and as it always will. Life eventually ensures that only what is in the highest good will continue and that all that is unbalanced will be transformed, either through the surrender and peaceful transmutation or through forced destruction and reorganization. Either way the result will be Life moving us back into balance.

Please understand I am coming from a place of peace as I speak about this inevitable process. And there is nothing to fear because no matter which way we transform as individuals or as a society, all will be as it should be. You can reduce any fear you may feel and any suffering you may endure as you go through this transformation by beginning *The Practice* of living Life from a place of unconditional love, acceptance, peace, and compassion. Then your thoughts and actions will benefit those around you and extend out for the highest good of all creation.

Highs and Lows

Figure 1 represents the general axis of Life experience. I'll be using this graph to demonstrate high and low fluctuations in energy and their potential physical, emotional, and spiritual outcomes. I am attempting to use a figure to demonstrate a process, so please remember that there are inherent limitations.

Let's define the zero point on the axis as a space of peace, that place of complete surrender, unconditional love, acceptance, and nonjudgment; this is the only space all creation can share in common. We can get to this place when we live nearly 100 percent of the time in *The Practice*, living Life moment by moment for the highest good of all.

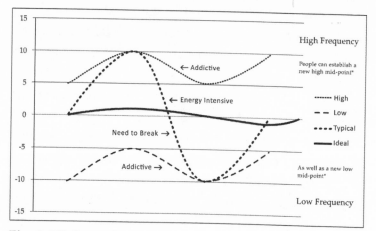

Fig. 1. Highs and Lows

Let's define the relative space above the zero point as *excessive* energetic imbalance (based on reaction to a Life experience), and the relative space below the zero point as *deficient* energetic imbalance (based on reaction to a Life experience). Excessive imbalance is perceived as positive and attractive while the deficient imbalance is perceived as negative and repulsive.

The degree of fluctuation above or below the zero point is based on each individual's subjective perception; each person's highs and lows will depend on their personal interpretation of the moment.

Excessive energetic imbalance would include perceived emotions such as the tenseness of fear, the high from caffeine and sugar, the thrill of excitement, or the stress of anxiety, for example. Excessive imbalance can also occur from "falling in love" as well as from setting a goal based strongly on time.

Examples of deficient energetic imbalance would be depression, fatigue, fibromyalgia—and generally what we think of as "sickness." The truth is that the presence of sickness or dis-ease is nothing more than the presence of imbalance that can be triggered through excessive *or* deficient energetic imbalances. Sickness sometimes happens to return the organism to balance. "I am sick" is merely the subjective label we put on one portion of our experience. As an example, when you are exhausted, you don't want to admit that it might be because you drank too much coffee or ate too many pastries. We lie to ourselves because we don't want to admit the truth that the low we experience (exhaustion) might have been the result of the caffeine high. We want the highs, but we don't want the lows that the highs trigger. Yet, imbalance always has to be brought back to balance.

We don't want to see that our excitement—generated by our thoughts of anticipation—has an outcome we often call "sickness." Excitement is good! If that excitement is too great, that energetic imbalance can lead to sickness or dis-ease in order for balance to be restored.

On a physical level, every time you enter into an excessive energetic imbalance, you are stimulating your body, relatively speaking, into a sympathetic dominant state. This engages the limbic system, which is a region of the brain that is affiliated with strong emotion and survival, and you experience a fight or flight response. This fight or flight response is very energy intensive and the body gives it top priority over any other situation going on. These states of high or excessive energetic imbalance lead to more wear and tear on the body and our being. The more the fight or flight response is engaged, the less energy and resources the body has available to cope with what it knows is in the highest good.

The limbic system, in turn, activates our endocrine system, including the hypothalamus, pituitary, thyroid, adrenals, and pancreas, which directly or indirectly affect blood sugar, blood pressure, metabolism, and sex hormone production, to name some of the bodily functions affected.

Is it any wonder that these repetitive energetic states of imbalance affect every system in our bodies? Our systems become taxed from being overworked and in a state of hyper-function. At some point, they will fail to function, or they will become hypo-functional, functioning at far less than an optimal level. Although I've noted some major body systems, all systems are affected in one way or another by the effects of repetitive energetic imbalance. It's a major reason why dis-ease appears in our physical form.

Your form, or body, will eventually manifest, to a large degree, your life experiences and the energetic imbalances you have allowed to affect it. Your body will mimic your life; the two are inseparable.

Remember, your thoughts affect your body. What you think about, you put your body through. Thinking takes energy. Do you see that your body has already paid the energetic price and the associated physical price of all the stress and anxiety you go through around your expectations of an upcoming event—which sometimes never happens? Thinking takes energy and affects every system in our bodies, so we have to ask: How much thinking can we really afford, when the result of thinking is usually just more thinking, creating imbalance in our systems?

I urge you to focus on balance, on living from the zero point, on living without the emotional fluctuations. It's also true that if we don't focus on sickness, it will eventually cease to exist to a large extent. We won't need it anymore to balance our system, to teach us. Furthermore, we will come to recognize that when sickness or dis-ease comes, it is but a sign that we need to restore balance in our lives. How can we call something that helps us "sickness"?

How do we avoid the yo-yo of balance/imbalance? If you are concerned or excited about a new job or a big presentation you are giving at work, don't let yourself get over-stimulated or over-excited. When you anticipate and push your thoughts and feelings into a future that hasn't happened, you will experience stress.

Whether in your business or personal life, come to

every moment and every experience from a state of peace. Relax. Take the emotion out; do what you're supposed to do in the moment. Trust that everything will go the way it's supposed to go. Allow the divine order to unfold.

I want to explain more about how these energetic imbalances affect your form or body. Every time there is an upward fluctuation of movement, regardless of the reason, it requires energy. The greater the reaction the greater amount of energy required. It requires energy to have a reaction. Consequently, the greater the amount of energy needed to react, the greater the chance you will find yourself in a state of excessive energetic imbalance. Every time there is imbalance, you have to be rebalanced or brought back to homeostasis, to the zero point—and that too takes energy.

The downward fluctuations of (deficient) energy are intensive in much the same way as a car brakes while going downhill. Either way, the overall process of living then becomes either generating energy to have a reaction or generating energy to recover from a reaction.

For example, if you speed while driving on the highway, you are purposely putting yourself in a situation in which you are going to be anxious and nervous about driving over the speed limit. You put yourself under continual stress in the hope of saving time, but the time you will save is not worth the damage you will do to your body. Or, if you find yourself stuck in traffic, you may become angry or stressed because traffic is not moving fast enough and now you will be late for an appointment. Yet you have no control over the situation. Why do we allow ourselves to have extreme emotional reactions over situations we can't control? In truth, we have no control over our outer environment at all. We can only control our inner environment.

To use another analogy, we can get better mileage by not over accelerating at the green lights and then riding our brakes at the red lights—and doing that over and over again. Remember that all these situations are relative moments of Life, and there are an infinite number of these moments. Each moment—red light or green light—is an ongoing process in the infinite field that is Life.

Look again at figure 1. The first observation we can make is that we don't usually spend a lot of time at the zero point—the point of peace. There is little or no space for constant peace because you only cross through that zero point in very small increments of time, very brief moments of time, relatively speaking, compared with the time you spend out of balance. So what this means is that many of us don't live efficiently from the space of the zero point—in peace. Instead, we live emotionally, react energetically, time and again, working to recover the highs, dreading the lows, up and down, over and over.

Mathematically speaking, there is a very low probability that even one person can experience the zero point of peace very often, let alone that two or more people can experience it together at the same moment, let alone a society, let alone a whole planet.

The ultimate questions are: Can you afford the energetic "bill" of being emotional? Can you afford to live, energetically speaking, beyond your means? If you are living beyond your means monetarily, for example, you are living beyond your means in the way I describe above. If you are suffering from some type of dis-ease it has most likely come into your life because you have been living beyond your means.

To correct the situation, begin living within your means, lower your fluctuations, stop spending energy you don't have, stop having reactions you can't afford, and start surrendering the personal choice to have those emotional highs. Literally, spend more time "at peace," conserving your energy for healing and the restoration of balance. Encourage those around you to do the same. This will bring well-being to you and all of Life.

Why?

It's important to understand why we continue to live beyond our means, unable to afford our emotional reactions or fluctuations that produce such energetic imbalances. You can increase your awareness so that you more quickly realize when you are living beyond your means. How do you begin to surrender to peace?

The true purpose of *The Practice* is to practice such surrender every moment of your life. So if you find yourself emotionally worked up, you will know that you forgot to surrender. Energetic imbalances will remind you that you need more practice. As I said, it's a process and either way, it's all good. Life will give us opportunities to practice, of that we can all be sure. Life will let you know how you are doing in *The Practice* by its uncanny ability to bring you the very moments you most need to practice.

Remember that the upward fluctuations of energy are primarily driven by fear and/or expectations. Nothing takes us into a space of boundless preparation and energy expenditure more than something we want, something we are excited to have or intent on becoming, or something we've become attached to and fear we might lose, especially to death. We can lose all connection with balance and therefore peace when we fear something or expect something. Time and again we engage in fear and/or expectation. If we get what we want, we then have to fear it will fall apart; we may have to watch it fall apart again. And, if what we fear losing we lose, then we spiral into emotional devastation and grief.

Why? You know the answer: because we have been under the control of our ego-based emotions, which are trying to prove they are right, that they will get what they want because they know best, and they have all the answers!

We have been parented—figuratively and literally—to believe this. We have been encouraged to take full responsibility for making our futures happen, to get what we want to achieve and accomplish our goals. From the time we were little children, we have been praised for doing so. Yet, now we know that to do so means that we bankrupt our peace and throw ourselves into imbalance. And we do it to ourselves many times. The momentary high we achieve, we lose again and again.

Our addiction to feeling up, happy, great, successful, accomplished, intelligent, etc. is unsustainable, and we cannot afford it. It leads to an ongoing addictive cycle during which we get ourselves or someone else "up" and then compete with ourselves or others to stay "up." But even if we win and stay "high," we lose our balance. Life will come along and rebalance us and we will eventually end up "down," in a cycle of energetic deficiency such as depression, discouragement, exhaustion, or dis-ease. It's inevitable.

As we hit rock bottom once again, we start wondering how we got there? We resolve to do better next time, and so begin the cycle again because *we know no other way to live.*

Be careful at this point. Hitting rock bottom and being in that destitute place only makes the addiction to excessive energetic imbalance stronger and all the more alluring. In other words, being down easily triggers us to get into an excessive state again. The allure of the "up" state becomes a motivating factor to recover from the "down." We so hope that the next time will be different; undeniably, that is a false hope.

The biggest reasons for excessive downward emotional fluctuations, which lead you into energy deficient states, are attachments and your inability to detach from your own subjective expectations and perceptions of Life and the expectations and perceptions others have of you. For example, you might be attached to "caring" based on outcomes. Caring, in this sense, makes you think highly of yourself, makes you feel good, makes others admire you. If caring causes downward fluctuations and a lack of energy in you, it is often because you don't accept yourself unconditionally, which prevents you from being at peace. Rather, you keep trying to care, you keep trying to "hold on," which leads you deeper into energy deficiency as demonstrated in figure 1.

Hold on to what? Hold on to your idea of what should be happening, or what should have happened, who you should be, or who you should have been, what someone else should do or should be or should not be, etc. You hold on to your sense of control! And your sense of control is subjective judgment, arrived at through an emotional evaluation or reaction. You see, we really get attached to our feelings or someone else's feelings about us or about what is happening. If we want to be at peace, we cannot afford these attachments.

One of the most obvious signs of this human phenomenon is how we deal with death. We spend immense amounts of time, energy, and resources to keep people alive who are going—and sometimes want—to die. We tend to think that, emotionally at least, we shouldn't let them go. We cannot let go. As a nation we spend more resources for end of life care, in general, than we do at any other time in any person's life. We are still heavily motivated to avoid or prolong the emotional experience of death and loss. We spend resources when people are ready to leave this Life because we are attached to them—they help us stay "up"—and we cannot let go, so we are not at peace.

Our Issues with Death

This emotional pattern of dealing with the part of Life we call "death" is unsustainable. It is an emotional addiction that we cannot afford financially or, more importantly, energetically. Humanity has come to an emotional attachment to death that I call "the new normal"—prolonging Life as long as possible for emotional reasons. This new normal around death kicks in when we have prolonged highs or lows around death for extended periods of time. We establish a "new" normal as a way of coping with being "stuck" in a prolonged state of excessive or deficient energy around the death of someone we love. I've heard people describe this kind of energetic imbalance like this: "It was all I knew! It was normal to me."

This state becomes normal because we are unaware that we can let go of control and surrender enough to come to a place of real peace with death. Rather than coming to peace, we maintain the "normal" thoughts and responses and choices, but when we are out of balance, Life will rebalance us if we do not let go and surrender and come to true peace.

As we develop a higher level of intuitive awareness, we will accept death as a part of every moment of Life. If we practice peace in every moment, to balance our lives to the best of our ability, we won't need to "spend" as much to restore balance because our growing consciousness will refuse to allow us to enter that place of energetic imbalance. Then we will accept death as necessary and natural and we will allow it to happen without such emotional, financial, and energetic expenditures. At some point, we will embrace death and love it for the resolution and transformation it brings. I even venture to propose that death that is balanced in this way is more affordable on a monetary level, because balanced people are, by nature, okay with dying. They are comfortable with change, which is what death is, so they die more quickly and easily, lowering the associated costs that are usually spent on care to keep them alive.

The Way Out

I hope you can see that this pattern of excessive energetic reaction leads to increased levels of stress. Moreover they are hard to change; we seem naturally resistant to the very changes that are in our best interest. Resistance, of course, exacerbates our stress and the effects of stress, leading to premature degeneration.

Yet, honestly, "premature" is not an accurate term in this regard because so-called "premature" degeneration is very predictable based on the amount of time we spend in energetic imbalance and increased levels of stress, which includes the "ups" of smoking or drinking; the emotional habits of worry, anger, and frustration; and the spiritual habits of shame, guilt, sin, and distrust.

Exercise can help reduce the effects of energetic imbalance, as can meditating, getting enough sleep and relaxation, eating a healthy diet high in raw fruits and vegetables, and loving and being loved. You may not live longer—but then again, Life is eternal—yet these practices will certainly help you achieve the highest quality of Life of which you are capable.

What is most helpful, though, is to become aware of and monitor your emotional reactions and energetic fluctuations, let go of control, and surrender into peace.

For me, living a sustainable Life is all about balance, which is about allowing the divine order of Life to guide me, to live in peace with that order, doing what it asks, and taking what it gives.

Be an example of balance for those around you. In this way you will be following your purpose of living Life fully for the highest good of all.

∽ 7. ∼
APPLYING THE
INTUITIVE WAY TO LIFE

WE'VE TALKED ABOUT emotions and feelings, how to let them go, how to arrive at the place that you no longer use feelings to guide you. We've discussed how feelings stimulate energetic reactions that play havoc with your mind, body, and spirit, and how to stay balanced. In Chapter Two, I mentioned the importance of intuition in living and loving your life unconditionally. Let's examine intuition in a deeper way as it is going to play such an important role in the coming chapters.

As you know, there comes a point where many feelings become a liability and burden; they no longer benefit us. We've now let go of feelings and emotional reactions and all that energy of reacting to Life. So now what?

Let's try something different. Unlike feelings, intuition is absent of self-interest. Its intention is the greatest good for all in any and every moment. Intuition does not

∽∽

create reactive emotions no matter what is going on, what is happening, or the outcome of situations.

Let's apply intuition to a few more challenging moments in Life that threaten our peace, the moments that threaten to drown us in the drama of conflict, pain, and suffering, and kick us out of balance. These are important moments so I don't want to dishonor or discount them. They are the teaching moments in which we either love the most and move into harmony with or accept the least and suffer from.

When those difficult moments you resist (rather than love) come along, you put yourself at risk of dis-ease and sickness. *It will be better when . . . It will be okay if . . . It will all be better when this is over. ..* These are the phrases we use when we are trying to cope, trying to survive whatever Life has brought to our door. These patterns of reaction and resistance add weeks, months, years, or lifetimes to our spiritual evolution, as well as create suffering for us and for those around us.

Remember that the purpose of *The Practice* is to live and love Life unconditionally, not to merely survive it. There will always be major moments in Life that will forever challenge us—unless we love them and accept them as part of Life. Then Life will no longer have to bring us such major moments over and over again because we've come to peace with them. We've learned the lesson that we will *never* understand why some things happen. No matter, we've learned to love and accept whatever happens. And what-ever happens no longer throws us into a meltdown.

Living *The Practice* will help develop your intuition. I've delved into death and loss in a previous chapter—as one of the areas of Life that we resist most. I provided some examples of speaking honestly from your intuitive knowing. As we've become detached from nature and insulated within ourselves, we've learned to resist death because we no longer get torn apart by a wild animal—something that was a part of human life for a very long time. We need to remember that death and loss are good and necessary parts of Life.

So, it's important to get re-inoculated to the truth about death. What I've done is visualize a potential experience of loss and death—one that created fear in me even though it hadn't happened. So I visualized the very thing I feared.

I have two young boys. One is wise, aware, and thoughtful; the other is a total daredevil who keeps riding his bike into the street, jumping off high places, and generally being a typical risk-taking boy. For a period of time, I found myself tormented by the image of my daredevil son getting hit by a car and seriously injured.

I didn't want this fear, worry, and suffering to control me, so I visualized my son getting hit by a car while I watched. I visualized holding his injured body and I visualized him dying in my arms. I wept and felt sick inside. I deeply felt the loss of my son during that visualization. Yet, as I held my son in my arms, I allowed myself to move into harmony with the death of my son. I made a conscious effort to come to peace with my son's death.

When I came through that terrible emotional experience in the visualization, I realized that Life was still here and I was still alive. I remembered that my son and I would live infinitely. I came to peace with the fact that Life may take my son, and my torment dissolved. I still watched out for him and taught him good safety practices. But the truth is that anything I might do may not be enough to save him; he may still die.

Once something has happened, what good does it do to see it as "bad?" It's neither a functional nor an efficient way to live—and not at all peaceful. As soon as I've judged anything, including death, as "not good"—even my son's—I've set up a pylon that keeps me from living Life fully, keeps me afraid and not free. The more pylons in Life, the less freedom, the greater the potential for creating, fear, anxiety, and worry going forward. If we persist in seeing certain situations as "bad," then *we* are deciding which experiences we need to evolve rather than allowing Life to decide.

We already know we can't always prevent Life from falling apart. Finally, we have to admit, "I have no idea what's going on." Finally we surrender the perceptual way of living, of thinking we can prevent things from happening by our fear, our worry, and anxiety. Finally, we realize that we don't know and we have no idea what's going on or what's going to happen.

That's when we finally make the shift into *The Practice* and turn to intuition. As you develop your intuitive knowing, you too will be at peace with losing someone or something you dearly love. At some point, you too will "own" that sense of peace during loss and death because you are entitled to it, because you know that without death there could not be Life. You move through any and every moment of Life with minimal resistance and minimal suffering. You stop trying to make anything happen. Then you see that death is present in every moment of Life; you see that death *is* and always *will be* so you embrace death and give thanks for its part in Life.

As you become more of a student of Life and of *The Practice,* Life itself will increase your intuitive knowing—not because you chose to have it or you somehow earned it—but because Life always brings the open heart and the mind willing to change exactly what it needs to grow in consciousness.

Metaphorically, intuition is the river of Life. The river is flowing along and you are flowing along with it from a point of balance and from a place of peace. You are peacefully going with the flow downstream, no longer trying to swim upstream. You are flowing around the rocks without conflict, learning what they have to teach you, flowing, allowing the river of Life to lovingly transform you.

Another benefit of living with intuitive knowing and being in intuitive balance with Life is that you're open to the truth wherever it takes you. You don't allow your opinions of how Life should be and what form Life should take to influence you. You're not in denial about anything but open in the sense of letting go of your own opinions and embracing whatever Life brings. You are at peace.

If you're in a space of peace and then experience an illness and pass away, what then?

There you are, okay with it all! You realize that you were in a space of peaceful balance, so there was nothing else to do, nothing that could be done. You are present to your perceived death (for Life is eternal); you are peaceful. You accept your death as necessary for reasons that you will never know or understand. So there's no more worry or fear. Can you imagine that?

Using our intuition, we can overcome any emotional experience, any experience based in time, any personal choice—and sink into oneness with whatever Life brings.

Applying the intuitive way to all of Life including death and loss is not something that will help you alone. It's something you do for everyone around you. It's a light you shine on every person you meet—whether they know it or not. Living intuitively means you live for the highest good of Life, each moment. Living like this helps everyone.

The great intuitives of the past such as Jesus, Buddha, Gandhi, Moses, and Mohammed experienced the same two reactions from people: intense love from those who knew that their deepest intention was only for the highest good of all and utter ridicule and hatred from those less conscious, or unconscious, who perceived them as a threat.

So these great intuitives of the past were often seen as people who needed to be removed from society, got rid of. Other people put up pylons so they wouldn't have to get close to those great masters of the intuitive way so as not to get too close to a dose of that intuition. People feared intuition because they didn't understand it—and they needed to understand what it was before they could accept and love it. They felt responsible for getting rid of the intuitives who (they felt) caused their fear. Sadly, they missed an opportunity for the evolution of their souls.

One other point: Religion segregates us. As long as we believe in a religion that separates us from each other in all the ways religions have the potential to do, we cannot afford it. With all due respect to all those who hold a religious belief system, I'm not out to abolish religion but to put it into a larger context. Humanity cannot become unified in a space of religion. It has not worked. It will not work.

There is nothing wrong with religion if you embrace religion and its inherent limitations. I suggest we rise above religion into our intuition and put our religious beliefs in an intuitive context. Once you apply the intuitive knowing, you will see the divine truth in each religion and in all religions. Their stories and beliefs may differ but the heart of each religion is the same: love. In each religion, there is a truth. Above all religions is the absolute truth of Life.

When people ask me if I'm a religious man, I respond, "I am not in a space where a specific religion serves the highest good anymore." I'm not able to access my highest sense of truth when I "believe" in a religion.

Then again, I'm not in my highest truth if I believe that I'm different than you. Quantum physics has proven that we are all from the same vibration at the deepest level. We're all from the same source; whatever you want to call that source is irrelevant. We are all in Life together, in different spaces of consciousness, different spaces of evolution. But we are all the same, and intuition tells us so. It provides a way to accept that all of us are in the same space and share the same eternal goals of unconditional love, acceptance, peace, and compassion.

Love Life and the order within it. I call the initial Source of Life "God" that created and still creates Life, giving it divine order. Whatever "my" experiences have been in the past or will be in the future, I will at some point return to the beginning, to the source of Life where there will be . . . Life! Love the Source that some call "God."

It's a good idea if we can learn from one another's Life experiences. That way, one of us can go through an experience for the rest of us. And we all do this for each other. If we're aware of what one person is going through—and without judging the experience or empathizing with it— we learn from it, then, there may be no reason for us to go through the same experience—unless Life means for us also to go through it.

If we don't value the learning we can get from observing others, if this kind of collective experience is not observed attentively, then we'll have many unnecessary experiences that cause suffering, as we see happening now; those experiences are not in the highest good.

I want to be clear: Experiences are necessary because of the level of unconsciousness, and if the level of consciousness increases, those experiences may no longer be necessary.

Become more conscious and, therefore, more efficient in living Life by being intuitive first and perceptive second. Intuition can reveal amazing things. Take nature for example. Perceptually we see a tree or a flower, but our intuition shows us the Source of Life through nature in a new—but old—way. All of a sudden Life or God isn't some intangible source but becomes very tangible.

Another example: We know perceptually how our body functions, but our intuition sees the intricate beauty of the human body and the miracle of what we call our lives, the miracle that we are. We become in awe of the divine order, even of divine death and divine loss. We've surrendered completely. Our intuition tells us that we are no longer a separate self—even our bodies are no longer ours—we are just the energy that is Life.

Come now into your intuitive space. Now is the moment, and the moment isn't for one of us but for all of us. People have achieved intuitive knowing individually, but rarely as a group, as a **Community of One**. So I'm asking you to apply intuition to every moment of Life and encourage others to do so; they will see the peace in you, the light in you. Let's awaken all of us now at the same time. Let's not go back to sleep in unconsciousness, believing in random occurrences. Life intends only good.

As you continue *The Practice*, the choice to live intuitively or not will no longer be available. You won't have any other choice *but* to live intuitively, in truth and in light. You'll be conscious enough that you won't go back to living perceptually, back to using emotions as a guide with all that imbalance. You'll no longer see yourself and others as separate from Life, separate from each other, or separate from the Divine. Let's awaken to the divinity within and live from that intuitive space so that all beings may be awakened and inspired.

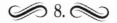

8.
RELEASING AUTHORITY
AS A STEPPING STONE
TO FREEDOM

I WANT TO EXAMINE a pattern of personal choice that emotionally affects us all: authority.

Let's define authority as the person, institution, or thing to which we give power over our lives. Authority is anyone or anything that we allow to define or control what is possible or probable for us. There are all kinds of authority, but each has the power to command us to do things, to influence our thoughts, and to determine what is right and what is wrong. Usually, the number of authorities we need in our lives is based on our level of consciousness; the less conscious we are the more authorities we believe we need.

We've all been kids and have experienced parental authority as well as various other authorities in our extended family, schools, church, or community. Growing up, one of our big motivations was that we didn't want to upset the authority—whoever it was—or disappoint him or her. We didn't want to aggravate the authority figures in our lives or get anybody mad at us. As adults, we continue this pattern by setting up other authorities. I'd like to discuss some of the suspects.

Let's start with our own ego, which has raised human intelligence to the level of an authority. We are confident that we know best. Even more, we've made ourselves into the ruler of the universe, proclaiming humans as ultimate messiahs of the planet. Our collective ego believes that *our* intelligence is higher than any other. Giving ourselves such an inflated authority has allowed us to discriminate against others who are different, whether by race, color, gender, culture, or religion. It has allowed us to design belief systems that make it okay to kill other humans and other forms of Life. Sometimes we call that authority "God."

As humans, we believe strongly in our intelligence, limited though it is. We believe so strongly in our human intelligence that we convince ourselves that some people are less important than others and should, therefore, be excluded from many ordinary behaviors—from sitting in a restaurant to marrying whom they wish, from being elected to a government office to being excluded from eternal Life.

We are in a situation now in which humanity has given itself authority over the planet and all other Life forms and organisms. After all, we've been given free will, haven't we? The authority we call God has given us free will as our birthright, right?

I'm not denigrating intelligence, but rather I'm questioning how we use it as an authority over other humans and other species like whales and birds and wolves. When we allow human intelligence to be the supreme commander of the planet, it becomes obvious that things aren't going well for many people and species. You've probably noticed that when humans run things, what is in the highest good is rarely mentioned.

How did we get this way? My intuitive hypothesis is that during a time of less consciousness, when we came up against events that were beyond our comprehension—such as death and natural disasters—we became so afraid that it seemed practical to take control of the overwhelming situations. We pitted our intelligence against infinite Life—and we see the results today. Yet we still think we're the greatest.

A growing consciousness is emerging, but it hasn't transformed enough of us yet. How soon do you think world leaders, church leaders, and business leaders will publicly admit "I don't know"?

I choose to believe this can happen in an instant. It is only a matter of moments before we all could be humbled by the unknown, incomprehensible infinite power of Life. In this next moment we could all admit that we don't know.

Our intelligence is limited and finite. It cannot offer answers to the most important questions that face us all: Why am I here? What happens after we die? Why did that tragedy happen? We've invented and turned to science and religion to investigate and answer these questions for us, or, at the very least, to provide a way to cope with the unanswered questions.

Science and religion both offer an explanation for how our universe came into existence. All religions provide very similar spiritual teachings to guide us about how to live together. But religions also have rules that we must follow—or we can't enjoy the "benefits" of that particular religious belief. There are rules of exclusion and inclusion—and they must be followed.

Certain religions, including Christianity, make God an authority in people's lives and put a lot of emotion around that authority, like guilt, shame, sin, and punishment. *If you do these things, you'll be good with God. If you don't do these things, you won't be good with God.*

I recently had a patient who came to me burdened by the authority of religion. He is a very intelligent man and he had studied many of the major religions without finding the freedom he thought believing and practicing the rituals of certain religions would bring him. He was struck over and over again by the rules, regulations, and proscriptions that even the least religious of the religions mandated. When I shared these teachings of *The Practice* with him, he said that he felt less burdened. He decided that what he needed to do to be free was to release himself from the authority he had given religion in his life. He then became Life's student and took Life as his authority.

Most of our standard authorities such as religion and science were initially created during a time when humanity was in a state of deeper unconsciousness; we needed more absolute authorities that would keep more of us from harming each other. But as a portion of us have evolved in consciousness, we have outgrown the usefulness of some of these authoritarian teachings.

Science and religion have a place, but just like our intelligence, we cannot give them absolute authority over our lives. They don't make us free, more conscious, or more mindful. They make us slaves. They make us tow the mark.

Although we're no longer children, we still don't want to upset or disappoint the authorities in our lives. How can we grow to be truthful when we don't want to upset an authority figure? How can we tell the truth when those emotions around authority are at stake? *Don't want to make it worse. Don't want to aggravate anybody. Don't want to be rejected. Don't want them not to like me.*

It's natural to react this way when we're ignorant of—or not conscious of—our true power. As we aspire to higher levels of intuitive truth, I can honestly tell you that you won't care what any "perceived" authority thinks of you.

Authority always thinks it's "right," but what it thinks is "right" may not be right for you. We all know people who do not let science or religion control their lives. Society thinks of them as oddballs or radicals. What must they base <u>their</u> lives on? We wonder.

Those people have likely become students of Life. They have found that it is possible to live a peaceful Life full of love, acceptance, and compassion without using religion, science, or their own personal—or the collective—intelligence as an authority. Without that triumvirate of authority, they can be moved instead by what is beyond their comprehension—Life. As a result, they are more willing to do what is in the highest good for all. They are more open to being guided by the divine order of Life. They are more free to do God's will, and they are not so hooked by whether or not others accept them.

Another big authority that most people realize has power over them is possessions. To a large degree our possessions control our lives. They can be handcuffs on your soul. The need or wish or drive to acquire things is, again, a man-made authority. The possessions we tend to think are most important are those society has sanctioned as good: important titles, big houses, big cars, beautiful bodies, a successful career, fame, and wealth. Technology is a new and powerful authority.

There's nothing wrong with any of these possessions—unless having them means we compromise the highest good. On their own, they signify a level of accomplishment and dedication. Does having such possessions signify that the highest good of all has been considered? Not necessarily. Often, it is quite the contrary. These possessions are accumulated not for the highest good of all but for the highest good of "me." Many people who are rich in possessions have missed, or are ignorant of, the eternal spiritual journey and the surrender it requires. They remain slaves to the authority of what they believe are their own accomplishments and the rewards those accomplishments have produced—their possessions. They have reached a false pinnacle and become complacent.

Many people believe that such desired possessions won't come into a life that is surrendered to doing only what is in the highest good from a place of peace, love, acceptance, and compassion. But they are mistaken. Possessions then become the simple byproduct of *The Practice* of living Life fully and unconditionally for the highest good. From a space of higher consciousness, we are more than ready to let such possessions go, if Life requires it. These people look to infinite Life as the only authority.

If you have an attachment to material possessions, you may *believe* the real authority in your life is your boss who makes you do something you don't want to do. But in reality, the real authority is the possessions you don't want to lose should you disobey your boss. In reality those possessions have become the authority in your life. They are keeping you in an unhealthy situation because their worth in your life has more authority than doing the highest good for all, for God, for Life.

There are certain situations in which we must accept authority—such as a work situation. In this case, for example, you don't accept your boss as authority over your whole life, but only during specific moments in your life that you are required to do something as a part of a job. If your boss asks you to do something you believe is unethical, you owe it to yourself to say *I do not agree with what you are asking me to do because I don't believe it is in alignment with the highest good. But you are my boss and I will do what you ask.*

Speak your truth kindly and politely but if you wish to stay at the job, do as your boss asks. When you reach a point where you are in conflict with doing something your boss asks of you, it probably indicates that the job is no longer in your highest good. You must rely on the order of Life to give you another job. You must leave, knowing it is in the highest good and trusting that Life will take care of you.

When you are fearful, you tend to stay in oppression. Fear leads to oppression. If you aren't full of fear, then you will go with the highest good and say to your boss, *I believe what you are asking me is to do is unethical. Is there another way to do it?* Give your boss the opportunity to think about the highest good. If he or she says "no," then tell your boss that you will have to consider your options.

People can become addicted to being an authority. The most godly people are humble and meek; they never speak of themselves as an authority. If we know who we are and what we are, we are immune to authority because we are not looking to be validated or to validate in that way. God's order within Life is our authority.

You see, authority is fine—until you become conscious enough to reject it.

No matter what position you are in, you are never a slave. We are all free—not free because of our choices but because being free to do God's will is our highest good. Yet, we often resist leaving authorities because leaving means changing our lifestyle—and that produces fear.

We need religion, science, our intelligence, and other authorities to guide us—until we don't. When you reach that moment of conscious awareness in which you know that the ultimate authority is Life, then Life moves, guides, and blesses you. Practice releasing all other authorities from your Life moment by moment.

True freedom comes from releasing our attachment to things we think we need or deserve or have worked hard to get. We need to re-think free will and personal choice as our operating systems.

I've come to the point that I don't really care if anyone likes me or not. It doesn't concern my daily activities or my life whether or not someone likes me. When you come to a place of complete love and acceptance, that game is over. You won't get into conversations with people wondering what you might say that will upset them. You will be authentic to the truth in every moment of your life to the best of your ability. At the same time, you will be deeply grounded in a space of love and acceptance.

There is and forever will be only one authority in my life—the divine order of Life—and the unconditionally loving force behind it I call "God." Through Life, God loves me unconditionally; if this were not so, I would cease to exist. Being in alignment with Life is my eternal goal. Unconditional love and acceptance are the tools I use to stay out of my own way. The result is deeper peace.

Take an honest and serious look at the many powerful authorities in your life. Evaluate them honestly. Crank up your intuitive knowing and allow Life to direct you. Your greatest freedom will come when you make Life your only authority.

I have an organizational structure in my practice, but there are no bosses. I am a steward of God's creation. We are committed as a group to doing what is in the highest good. We want everyone to be free to do that with us. Those that are ready to be in that space stay, and inevitably those that are not leave on their own accord, or are politely asked to.

When you are at peace with Life and you no longer need to continually look to appease others who were once in authority, you have begun to trust Life. It's important to always remember that you are free, that you do not have to stay in oppression and be a slave to it. Only you can decide, but we all know, intuitively, what is in the highest good.

∽ 9. ∽

FROM PERSONAL CHOICE TO CHOICE-LESS SURRENDER

WE'VE BEEN TAUGHT by our culture, religion, educational systems, and in many other ways, that human beings have "free will," that free will is one of our basic human spiritual rights. We think we are free to choose to do whatever we want to do, have whatever we want to have, albeit within the law. We think that free will means we are free, that we have true freedom.

Free will means that if we want a big car, a big house, the nice vacation home, the spouse of our dreams, and the big bank account, we will do what it takes to get those things. But we rarely consider the consequences.

The consequences of free will, which results in personal choice, affects others and the world around us. Free will doesn't have consequences only when we are completely ignorant of the effects of our personal choices. What we think, say, do, and have does affect others. Personal choice always has consequences.

I want to offer another perspective. I believe that living out of our free will, through personal choice, is only the illusion of freedom. We think we are in control, everything is going well, we have at least some of what we want—and then what happens? We get sick, and we wonder *What did we do wrong?*

We lose our job, our house, or our spouse and we wonder where we went wrong. *How did this happen?* This is the downside of free will. We think we can control Life and we get upset when we can't.

Letting Life decide also has consequences but we accept them as part of Divine Order, as opportunities to increase our level of acceptance of "what is." We don't see them as "negative" consequences. We accept them as being for our higher good and out of our control.

I believe God has given us free will so we can give it back. That's the choice we have! We give back our free will and personal choice and embrace choice-less surrender, which is very freeing. We move out of our egocentric orientation and we say, "I really don't know what is best for me or for anyone else or for the world. God, I just don't know. I only want to do what you want me to do."

That's real freedom—when we release the need to control our lives.

True freedom is living without judgment, without emotions as guides, without caring what others think of you, without all those emotional and energetic reactions that unbalance us. True freedom is intending the highest good, doing what God wants you to do—without fear. That is freedom.

If you operate from Thy Will, then you are free. No more burden of "why did I say that," or "why did I do that." You can be at peace with what you know and what you don't know, what you've experienced and what you haven't experienced. You are operating intuitively, connecting to the source within you, moving beyond your own self-judgment. You are amazingly free.

Free will isn't about freedom. Free will has consequences on us and others and it's burdensome. Our free will is trying so hard to get it right, to make the right decision, to achieve and succeed. Free will doesn't often think about the highest good. If you don't know what is in the highest good in a particular situation, then doing what you want to do is the best you can do.

We are all free to do what we want to do—to use our free will and personal choice until we become conscious of a higher good, and that consciousness grows strong in us. I don't want to minimize any choice we make because Life is an eternal process of increasing consciousness. When you operate from the space of your thinking mind, free will is the way to go. But then, what happens? We get sick—and wonder what we did "wrong" to bring on this sickness?

Contrast the way of free will with the intuitive way of choice-less surrender:

- Remember that Life is eternal.
- Affirm the truth that Life intends only good.

- Surrender to "Thy Will" acknowledging that you don't know what's best.
- Accept that you will never know or completely understand why things happen.

Since Life itself wants to teach you how to master the art of living fully and joyfully in peace, no matter what. If you come from a place of "Thy Will" then if you're sick, you're sick. You don't blame yourself. You know the sickness holds some kind of blessing.

Then if someone is having a problem, you are free to stay peaceful and joyous without thinking you did something wrong or you need to fix the problem.

The more you grow in consciousness, the more you will want to do what is in the highest good. When we realize that we don't always know what *is* in the highest good, we commit to choice-less surrender, to Thy Will.

The more you commit in this way, the more you almost *have to*. You find that it's not a burden, not so much a responsibility, as it is an honor bestowed on you by Life as directed by God. The more moments you have in choice-less surrender, the more consciousness increases naturally. Hence, "With experience comes wisdom."

As we grow in age, wisdom, and Life experiences, we lose our reliance on personal choice and our belief in free will. We come to a space of peace with Life just as it is. We welcome higher consciousness, we intend Thy Will, and we want what is only in the highest good for the greatest number. When change comes, we embrace it.

When we are in the space of relying on free will

and our personal choices, we usually don't react well to change; we tend to resist it. But that resistance means that we automatically escalate the number of moments needed to reach greater consciousness. Resistance always means that we suffer more and so do others.

Life understands that it has to teach us. No matter what you did, no matter what she did, no matter what went on, you are still one with Life. Life commits to us. No matter what they did to hurt you, no matter what they did to disappoint you, no matter how they abused you, you are still one with Life. That too is choice-less surrender.

There's a truth operating here: **Life in all its force and order will inevitably bring all of us into a greater place of consciousness, whether or not we consciously choose it, and Life will also resolve our unconsciousness.**

Over and over again, Life offers us the experiences and situations we need to grow in wisdom, awareness, surrender, and intuitive knowing. Time and again, Life will ask us to grow more fully into our intuitive knowing and into a higher consciousness. And what is Life's purpose in all this? It is to bring about the highest good for all Life, human and other. Isn't that something to be grateful for?

So if the intention of Life is so big and intends so much good, then our puny personal choices pale in comparison, don't they? When we really "get" this, we sink willingly into choice-less surrender now and in the future.

Let's think for a moment about how we deal with the future. We hypothesize about it, put expectations on it, hook goals to it, and then surround the whole thing with fear. Time becomes important when we think about the future, even though time is a human measurement invented to quantify Life —which is infinite and eternal. How can time measure the infinite, the eternal? Life is infinite and eternal and so are we. See how we choke the future with our free will and personal choice? See how we release it with choice-less surrender?

What about the present? We do all sorts of things to that too, put all sorts of thinking around it. Even when we say, "Now I'm going to the store . . ."—just like that, the moment *now* is past tense. But when we view everything through our sensory perceptions, the emotion around *now* gets picked up by our central nervous system which takes a hold of *now* and applies all sorts of data to it— such as how *this* now compares to *that* now, how what happened in the past might compare to *other* nows in the scary future. Then our brain judges *this* now as better or worse. After all this goes on, we react—mostly in fear—to secure our own survival, which creates high degrees of stress to the mind, body and spirit. It's energy intensive and creates imbalance in our system.

We don't know what it's all about! Why is that truth so hard to accept?

Rather than live so inefficiently with chaos and suffering as our partners instead of joy, I believe we do have another choice: *The Practice* of living intuitively from a space of unconditional love, peace, acceptance and compassion in choice-less surrender. *The Practice* encourages you to love Life on its terms, not yours, and to surrender your free will and personal choices for the greater good of all Life.

Life is not out to get us; it is out to bless us, teach us, heal us. Allow it, and it will even heal what ails you. Life will put an end to your suffering and lead you into greater peace, love, and fullness. Life will heal you. Use your free will to adopt choice-less surrender as your modus operandi. Turn to Life, to God with humility and gratitude and say, "Thy Will."

See yourself, others, everyone, and everything as Life. As you move more and more into choice-less surrender, you will have no choice but to love yourself, everyone, and everything. You and I are not humans first; we are Life first and eternally.

Never will you understand the magnificence that is Life—but that will no longer bother you. It will be okay because you've surrendered to Life's will. And what does Life intend? Only the good. This is *The Practice*.

Let's take the example of someone you love who is now angry at you. If you cannot unconditionally love and unconditionally accept this person's anger and you respond with anger, what is your first task? To unconditionally love and accept yourself in your disharmony.

- Then to remember that Life only intends the good.
- Then to remember Thy Will and to choice-lessly surrender, to learn the lesson Life is teaching you.
- Then to be grateful for the opportunity to unconditionally love and accept yourself and the other.

As you practice, over a greater and greater number of experiences and respond with choice-less surrender, responding in unconditional love will eventually become your first option.

I practice this kind of living moment after moment. As a student of Life, this is what I've learned and what you too will learn as you put yourself in Life's classroom as a student rather than a distracted observer. We are all at various levels of consciousness and we can all ask each other, humbly, to live without suffering by engaging in *The Practice* of living and loving Life from a place of unconditional love, peace, acceptance and compassion. We can do it to help ourselves, our families, our friends, our so-called enemies, and our world. The end of unnecessary suffering can begin right now, in each of our lives as we surrender personal choice, as we choose choice-less surrender and "Thy Will."

Then we can release our need for emotions to guide us and the energetic reactions they stimulate to unbalance us. We free ourselves and all others from unnecessary suffering.

As you move into choice-less surrender, what will you lose? For one thing, you'll lose the drama that always seems to be around our personal choices. You'll lose the kick of emotions and the stress of reactions. You'll lose hyperactivity.

Life becomes wonderful and beautiful and even. No more daily roller coaster rides. No more egocentric personal choices that amount to getting in your own way.

It won't be exactly monotonous because you will always be in a state of gratitude. Able to more fully witness the divine order of Life and learn from it, instead of reacting to it, trying to survive it.

Practice releasing personal choice every minute of your Life for the rest of eternity. Live out of *The Practice* of saying Thy Will and letting Life bring you exactly what you need to grow in consciousness. Allow Life to dictate all outcomes and release all personal attachment. Remember Life isn't personal—it's just Life.

This doesn't mean that we stop working and start just waiting for something to happen. We engage Life, exercise, pay bills, participate in our communities, spend time with our family, work. We engage with all of Life from a place of balance, without attachment, without caring how anything turns out, without trying to fix or control anything.

If something happens that is unpleasant or hurtful, we embrace it, accept it unconditionally, learn from it, and allow it to bring us to a higher space of consciousness. We didn't cause it—because we have surrendered to choice-less-ness—so if Life brought it to us it must be in the highest good. We are free to relax with whatever it is. We are free to end suffering—our own and the suffering of others. We are no longer afraid of death because if Life brings it, it must be in the highest good.

Hang on to the illusion that personal choice is the way to go. I hung on to it for a long time. Discover for yourself where peace is. Is it in personal choice or is it in choice-less surrender? You decide. Another way of asking the question is: Where is the fear and chaos—in personal choice or in choice-less surrender?

Believe me I lived for a long time in the space of believing I was making things happen or not, keeping things going, keeping a marriage going, keeping a job going, keeping friendships going—that illusion of control.

The Practice offers a peaceful, moment-by-moment process of practicing unconditional love, acceptance, and compassion. It opens us to a space of complete surrender, letting Life decide what's going to happen, what's not going to happen, who will stay and who will go.

I believe that God gave us free will so that we could give it back through choice-less surrender. Rather than saying "I want" and "I will," we say "Thy Will." We grow in *The Practice* of loving and living Life unconditionally by saying moment by moment "Thy will." We let Life bring us what we need. We stop making it all happen. We let go of fear and move into choice-less surrender.

Therein lies true freedom.

THE POINT
OF NO RETURN

STAY IN A SPACE of stillness as I share with you a story that, for me, was profound and metaphorical, awakening the intuitive in me.

It was a clear night, and I was sitting outside. Earlier, I'd watched a beautiful sunset but now the sun had set and the air was crisp, clear, cool, and refreshing. There wasn't a cloud in the sky. As I looked up into the clear, night sky, I saw an endless abyss of stars. I'd seen this sight many times and, although it never ceased to amaze me, this night it held a new lesson. In that moment, I heard God speak within me.

"Do you understand the purpose of day and night?" God asked. "Do you see that day and night are more than a physical process marking the end of a day and beginning of a night?"

Everything within me awakened, and I said, "Yes, I understand."

I understood in that moment that the blue sky we see on any given day is nothing more than a reflection of the water molecules as the sun hits them. The *blue* gives us the incredible illusion that the infinite, black sky is not out there. We experience this illusion for hours every day. But the *blue* sky does not really exist. Only the black infinite sky is out there.

I believe that "blue sky" is a God-given perceptual "break" from the incomprehensible infinite reality of the universe, of which we are but one tiny part. I think God gives us this blue-sky illusion because if we were forced to face that black infinity on an ongoing basis—especially when we are not fully conscious—it would be too much to handle.

"Blue sky" is kindergarten consciousness; it represents a state of ignorance. We all start there, and some of us live our whole lives believing that blue-sky illusion. As we spend more and more time in Life's classroom, we realize that there is a purpose to the blue sky and a purpose to the inky, night sky.

I realized that believing in that blue sky made me feel comfortable, loved, and appreciated. Who doesn't love a blue sky? It makes us think that all is well and we are safe. But it's an illusion. How do we come to terms with the truth that the sky is really infinite blackness? How do we become comfortable with that infinite, black space, with that unknown, ever expanding universe?

What I've done is become comfortable with the fact that, in a physical sense, within that space of infinity, I am nothing. If it takes the light from a star millions of light years to reach me, the sheer distance it must travel boggles my mind; I cannot comprehend it. But that night sitting outside looking into that dark ever expanding universe, I became comfortable with my insignificance. I realized that the purpose of the blue sky was to give me a break from the purpose of the night sky, which was to show me who I am.

Try to stare at the night sky universe and accept it on its terms. Be ready to see—not only what is apparent to your eyes—but also that which is hidden and far beyond your comprehension. Be open to messages and truths that come from a place you and I cannot fathom, describe, or understand.

At one time, anything that could not be physically substantiated by the senses or understood by the human mind was considered the "dark" side. The dark created fear. But now we know that the dark, ever-expanding universe is the *truth* of things—not the illusion of blue sky. Think about this—and practice amazement. Sit with the dark night sky as I did; smile at its lessons. Understand the beautiful truth and humor that it is all dark space, ever expanding. It's all unknown.

As you embrace the dark reality of infinite space, your intuition will deepen. As a result, you will become more comfortable with *what* you are: a speck of matter in a dark and infinitely expanding universe. None of us will ever completely understand our experiences in this dark and infinite universe.

As your intuition deepens, you will have moments, as I do, in which you will want to close that newly developed intuitive eye, and bring back that comforting blue sky. There will be times when you will try to convince yourself, *"No, it's all blue sky. This is all there is. It's about going to work, making a living, and raising a family, and that's all. This planet Earth is all there is. The idea that other life is out there is a joke. This planet and the blue sky—that's it. See that blue sky? Right here is where all the answers are. It's all contained right here, under the blue sky. Life isn't infinite. There are no other life forms out there having similar experiences to ours; surely we have nothing in common! We are alone. All alone."*

But when that intuitive eye is open and alert, we face the reality that we are a speck of dust floating amidst an infinite number of specks of dust in a black, ever-expanding universe. You accept that the *why* of most of your experiences is and will always be unknown to you; you don't understand it and nobody else understands the why of their experiences either.

The true force of Life, which I call "God," is invisible much of the time. But that force makes *matter* what it is. Many questions arise: Does the universe in and of itself have order? Is there an order that began the universe? Did matter come first or did the force that created matter come first? Was evolution brought about by the nature of the things created or by an external force?

The way I understand it, there is an initial force of order behind all matter that brought matter into existence. There wouldn't be matter unless there was a force that created it. Think of this as an analogy: the boxcar at the end of the train does not move on its own; it needs an engine. To me the engine of all the organization in the universe is Life, or God, which creates form out of matter. Life or God makes matter *matter*. God creates form out of matter.

We can doubt and resist this truth and create another illusion similar to the blue sky. We can say WE are God. But, in truth, we are *of* God just as matter is *of* God. As compared to religious and scientific views, the spiritual view asks: Did creation arrive completely out of nothing and if it did arrive out of nothing what force or intention brought it out of nothing? Isn't there an intention or force that brings even our ideas into existence?

Does the type of atom or matter that Life or God created give it the ability to bond with other atoms? Yes, but that ability to bond is given by what created matter in the first place—Life/God.

So matter, by itself, cannot and does not create itself. The force of Life that creates matter also gives matter form and the ability to change form. As you embrace the intuitive way—the way of unconditional love, acceptance, peace, and compassion—you will look at the night sky as the true reality and you will become comfortable with how much you don't know. From that realization, you will live your life knowing that on a blue-sky day, you will choose to live from the reality of the night sky, with the deep intuitive knowing that you are a speck of dust among millions of specks of dust expanding in an ever-expanding universe.

This is the point of no return—the point at which you become conscious enough to know that you are one with all things. Living in duality is over. You *know* that your life is nothing more than a drop in the ocean. This is the point at which you become conscious of your unity with all matter. It's no longer about "you" and your answers; you give up control that you will ever make sense of it all. It's beyond the point of having all the answers and being in control—all those fallacies.

Don't stay at this point of no return. My advice is to move past this point of no return, of emptiness, and completely fall in love with the unknown darkness of the infinite black sky. Embrace the darkness and the unknowningness within you. Surrender to something so beyond that you cannot comprehend it, but you love it and embrace it anyway because it is the force of Life. It is God.

The night sky, as astronomers have shown us, has a marvelous synchronistic force and order. Living Life from the reality of the night sky means that we allow all moments—which are infinite—to touch us intimately. These moments are the presence of God—they are God being intimate with us.

Eventually, we learn to become aware of how these unseen forces move and shift, what kinds of patterns they have, what kind of order and purpose. We sit in Life's classroom and study. Eventually, we become comfortable with the unseen and the infinite, and the unknown forms it may take. Leave behind the perceptions of the world that you were so sure of when you were not as conscious.

We can't live all the time in the place of this truth. We let it go and look at the blue sky. But we remember the reality of the black unknown infinite sky. We remember God's force and intimate presence beyond that blue-sky illusion.

As a start, let this truth help you make small but important changes. For example, let's stop using "old" and "getting older" to define ourselves. Those terms are as inaccurate as the blue sky we think of as real. Just as blue sky is an illusion, so is time, which is a human-created illusion. As we let go of more and more illusions, the following truth becomes apparent: **Every life form constantly undergoes change as a natural result of the order within the field of Life.**

The deepest intention of Life is to create and change form so that consciousness continues to increase and resistance to Life in all its manifestations continues to decrease. As we become more conscious and lessen our resistance to change, we accept that Life has an order and a force, and we surrender to it.

When we move from the illusion of blue sky as our comfort and safety to the reality of the unseen forces of the dark and infinite universe, we have released our need to be sure of anything; we have released our need to control our lives. We surrender to the unseen forces of Life and its creator.

Humans, trees, plants, other animals change form constantly. You are not the same form as you were at six months old or even six months ago. When we turn one year old, what a party people give us. *"Wow, look at you,"* they say. *"Wow, now you're walking. Now look at you—you're riding your bike. Look at how big you're getting. Wow, you're turning into a nice young lady. Now, look at you carrying a child inside you. . . "*

Then right around that forty or fifty year old mark, which is when we begin to describe ourselves as "old" and "getting older," and create issues around age because, ignorantly, we believe in the aging process and in the degeneration of our bodies, our form. In our culture, getting older has a negative connotation. But here's the truth: If *we* are getting older, then *Life* is getting older. We are a speck of Life itself. And if we keep perceiving getting older as negative, we will resist this natural rate of change—and through resistance, accelerate the rate at which we grow older. Why stop celebrating? Even when we do celebrate age as a triumphant accomplishment, we usually don't celebrate the changes in our body that got us there.

Some people become hyper sensitive to the changes in their body. Instead of embracing the changes with love, acceptance, and peace, they dread them. All of a sudden, our world that was full of infinite, ever expanding possibilities becomes a small, blue-sky illusion again. When you begin to dread and fear the aging process, you are no longer living from your true place in the dark infinite universe; you are living from the blue-sky illusion, again believing the illusion that you are defined by your bodily form.

Our souls are infinite. Our bodies change because Life changes all forms. Life itself changes. Why resist it or dread those changes? I believe we need to accept change as a result of the force of Life, which affects everything, including us. Let's not identify your soul which is infinite with your form that is naturally changing. If we are getting old, then so is Life. When we embrace this truth, we save ourselves unnecessary suffering.

Trees are a beautiful example of not resisting change. Every fall, the unforeseen forces and order of Life brings a change of color to their leaves. Then as winter, their most challenging season approaches, the trees do not hang on to their leaves, they let them fall. Trees allow the loss; they go with it. They don't resist. What happens next? Their nonresistance brings a springtime of new birth.

Sure some oaks and other trees do hang on to their leaves, but in most cases a tree that holds on to its leaves when that species usually lets them fall indicates that the tree is unhealthy. We are meant to lose our "leaves" as well, and we are meant to do it over and over again, going through a shedding and through a change of form. Forever, we will be going through a change in our form because we are forever a part of Life—the infinite field of Life—which is forever.

Change is a constant sign of the presence of God. Can you think of wrinkles as a sign of God's presence? They are! All change is a sign of the infinite. Changes in our bodies and form are beautiful, especially when they are unimpeded and unresisted. As you follow the lessons in

The Practice, you will find yourself enjoying all that Life and God have to offer you in the way of experience and change.

Awhile back, I began to notice that I was losing some of my hair (as if I haven't always been losing hair). In an attempt to surrender to what I thought of as "the worst case scenario," I cut my hair very short. I looked into the mirror until I could say, "So what!"

We need to disempower our fear of our bodily form changing or the fear will control us. It will control what we are capable of being and becoming; it will control how quickly we become conscious. As I suggested in an earlier chapter, harmonize with a possible future experience that bothers you, worries you, or concerns you – something you dread. Just bring yourself to that situation, like I did in cutting off my hair, or visualize your fear happening as I did with my son getting hit by a car. When we harmonize with what we fear might change, we are disempowering fear, no matter what it might be about. Change is constant, the only true constant. Might as well embrace it.

Every day, whether we admit it or not, our bodily form is changing. I now love my form, whatever form that might be. Come to the place where you do, too. Be happy to have a body, but don't allow it to define you, because if it does, then you will have no peace in your soul as it changes. Practice living Life so that all the resistance is gone. Take it all out. Let go the whole idea of bodily form around which our culture places so much emphasis. As your life becomes more and more balanced, honest, peaceful, what else can you do but accept change, learn from it, love it, embrace it, live it. And remind yourself every day that it's going to change.

Your life also has a form. Each of our lives has a certain form, a certain context, a structure, a repetitive quality. What form is your life taking right now?

So what will the form of your life do? Change, of course. As you observe your life, you notice that it changes from minute to minute. We barely notice this continuous momentary change because we are still in blue-sky thinking where everything is defined and under control. But in every instance, in every time, the truth of Life is what is beyond the blue sky. It's the same with our physical bodies and it's the same with the form of our lives. It's all in flux, all the time.

So what you consider to be a surprise in your life, I consider to be the very thing that needs to happen next. We may never know why it had to happen—but that's an irrelevant question. Continue to open so you can see the continuous change and order of Life more clearly. When you no longer rely on emotions or our blue-sky notions of time as guides, and when you no longer resist aging, death, or loss, you will come to a place of peace with Life. And that place will amaze you.

How about the "form" of your beliefs? Your beliefs change like your body changes and the form of your Life changes. When we don't allow our beliefs to change or the form of our lives to change shape and when we resist our bodily changes, we are believing that the blue sky is all there is—that it's not an illusion, that we are in control.

The world is full of people who do exactly this. They are desperately trying to hold on to the idea that nothing changes, and they suffer incredibly as a result. But their suffering is not going to prevent change. We can release the authority of old beliefs now that we know who we are and we can live from the infinite universe.

There is an incredible lack of density in the universe. There's way too much space for everything not to continue to expand. We cannot be contained—there's too much space. We are primarily surrounded not by matter but by space.

Someday you will look at that infinite universe and say, *The universe is me and I am the universe. I am what the universe is and it is what I am.* What else could you say? If the universe is full of space and expansion, so are you, for you are a small part of it.

Our planet came from that universe and is a part of it, and our form comes from this planet. We are *of* that starry sky. When you can accept that truth, you realize that form is irrelevant. Think of it this way: I will be in one form or another forever, because I am the "I am" and you are the "I am", and we will be in one form or another forever.

Some forms you may like, others you may not. *The Practice* is about loving them all throughout this Life or for an eternity; on some level, it's all the same experience. So fall in love no matter your form, no matter what form your life takes, no matter what form—or no form—your beliefs take. Eventually each form will change because Life keeps changing.

So I'm jogging on a beautiful day. I have run the same route before, from my office down to Edgewater Park, out past Wendy Park to the Coast Guard station on the shores of Lake Erie, and then back to my office. The sanitation is along this route, and when I first ran this route, the smell from the sanitation department was overwhelming. It was just like s!?t. No other word fits; it literally smelled like s!?t. On my run that day, I breathed very shallowly as I passed the sanitation department, trying not to let the smell affect me. I was happy to get past it.

On the return loop back, I had to pass through that s!?t again. I saw the sanitation department ahead. Suddenly I sensed God speaking. (It has been one of the profound characteristics of my life that God teaches me something when I need it.) I hear the inner voice of God asking me, "Why did you try to stop breathing when you ran through that air by the sanitation department?"

"Because it smelled like s!?t," I said.

"You are of the same origin as that s!?t," God said.

Then I realized the truth: *Oh my God, I am from the same elements as the s!?t.* What is in it, is in me. Its chemical bonds are the same as mine; its carbon molecules are no different than mine. Why do I believe I have the right to judge and label it? Those microscopic forms of Life producing that odor benefit from the same field of Life as I; they too have to be here.

Then God said to me, "On your run back, you must embrace that. You must breathe that with greater acceptance. If you don't, you will always see it as something separate from you, something that either you are *above*, or it is *beneath* you. You must embrace every part of Life as necessary and as equal, even though you don't understand why. That smell is there because I allow it to be there—for a reason, and you must embrace it completely. Otherwise, you will separate yourself—by an illusion of choice—from part of Life."

Wow, I thought. So I ran back past that sanitation department, and I breathed, deep running breaths. I'm not going to lie to you because even though I knew that what God said to me was profoundly true, I wasn't completely comfortable. It smelled!

But I made an important shift that day. I recognized that I saw that there was still a part of me that held on to the same blue-sky thinking that I wasn't part of the s!?t, that it wasn't me! I surrendered right then and there. I breathed the smell in and I harmonized myself to it. I was glad I did.

It was awhile before I ran that route again, but when I did, the smell didn't bother me in the least. I was past the sanitation department before I even realized that I had come through that smelly section of Life without noticing it. I didn't think about it being smelly. That's what less resistance does—it takes the suffering out of everything.

We all have s!?t in our lives in one form or another. Things stink, and you don't want to accept them, you don't like them. You want to judge and label them as bad or wrong, as s!?t. These are old patterns of ignorance related to the blue-sky illusion. Once you "get" this illusion, you know that it's just stuff that doesn't smell good. It's Life in a different form. It's in another Life form that's moving up to a higher level Life form.

It's just Life. Don't give it a negative label that brings about fear or resistance, judgment or condemnation. Don't give it a negative word, like "old," "sinful," "s!?t," or "evil." It is what it is, otherwise it would be something different. Anything that is a part of Life is a part of you and me, is a part of God. Nothing is outside Life or God.

People want to put certain events and situations *outside* God so they can believe that God is who they believe God to be. This is blue-sky reality because if you, I, and the universe are expanding infinitely, so is God because nothing is outside God, which is Life. But I mean it when I say that it's okay if you are not yet ready to live from the starry infinite night sky.

If you choose to live from your intuition, in a space of unconditional love, peace, and acceptance, then think about the meaning of "unconditional." It doesn't mean we love it until . . .until it smells bad, until she has cellulite, until he has wrinkles. Unconditional means unconditional. Living this way is how you can best get along with an infinite field called Life, forever! If we're going to "get along" with something that we're going to be a part of forever, there can be no conditions on our love for Life.

It's a good thing that Life is a good teacher because we're going to experience these same situations over and over until we stop realizing we're running by the sanitation department. We stop labeling anything as s!?t. We enjoy every moment along the way and consider it all a part of the journey, all a part of the experience. We love it all, unconditionally.

But you won't experience this kind of love until you start looking past the blue sky. Blue sky is a nice break from reality; everyone loves blue skies. But you'll only see the real deal when the sky is dark and infinite. That is the universe we live in. When you keep that perspective, you can enjoy the blue sky. But you never forget what's behind it.

I'll close this chapter with a story from my healing practice. A wonderful man who I will call "Adam," who was diagnosed with pancreatic cancer came to see me. He had been told that he had five months to live. He told me that he came to see me because, after all, he's coming to see everybody right now. "I just want to go through this experience with some dignity, and with some quality of life," he said.

"Adam," I said. "I need you to accept a basic truth, if there is anything I can do to help you."

"What basic truth?" Adam asked.

"How do you see yourself? How do you define yourself?" I asked him.

He sat there struggling with the questions. "Who asks me these kinds of questions?" he said.

So I walked him through it. "Do you believe in a force of Life," I asked. "Do you believe there's something that gives us the force of Life?"

"Yes," he said.

"Are you okay with me calling that force of Life God?"

"Yeah."

"So you agree with that," I said, looking at him. "And do you believe that you are in a form we call human form?"

"Yeah," he answered again.

"So do you see any argument with calling yourself a result of the God force in human form? You are God in human form. You are the product of the force of Life, the source of which is coming from God manifesting itself in a human form. Do you know that to be true in this moment? Can you accept that?"

"Yes," he said. "But doesn't that sound pompous?"

I could see he still had some blue sky in his reality. To call himself God in human form violated a bunch of really big rules. So I said to Adam, "If the truth is pompous, then the truth is pompous. Maybe we're all really underestimating ourselves, because we can't believe a simple truth, that we are part of Life, of God."

Adam realized this truth. I also taught him several teachings from this book, about emotions and feelings not being good guides to live by, about refusing to be the victim of other people's feelings. As Adam lay on the exam table, I could not put my hand on his stomach because the pancreatic cancer was causing him such pain. He couldn't even touch his own stomach without pain. He was on morphine and OxyContin for pain. Even so, the pain was so excruciating.

By the end of the visit, Adam was pressing on his abdomen and breathing deeply, free of pain. Yet, when he left, it wasn't the relief from pain that he was most grateful for. "Thank you so much for just taking the time to help me see these things," he said. He was talking about his realization that he was part of Life, of God.

When you live the teachings of *The Practice*, it will become apparent in your life and you too will be able to articulate these teaching so they help others. You will be an example of that which you truly are.

When Adam walked out of my office, I said, "I'd like to see you in a few days."

"I've got to tell you something," he said. "I've gone to see several doctors and walked out of their offices completely overwhelmed."

I realized he was referring to sensory overload; he was overwhelmed by perception, emotional reactions, what they do to the body.

"And I'm walking out of your office today." Adam continued, "completely overwhelmed, but in a completely different way. I am overwhelmed by a peace right now."

Does it really matter, at this point, what happens to this man's form? No, because all the pressure is off him. He's focusing on his relationship with Life, his relationship with the giver of Life, God. Within an hour, he's touching his stomach. He may still die soon, but death is an inevitable eventuality for every form. Adam was an example of how *The Practice* can help you find peace and dignity for the rest of your life. Regardless of what Life may hold, these teachings give us a way to experience Life with a high level of quality and dignity. Try it. Look past the blue sky of your own death. Go through it, embrace and experience it with a sense of quality and dignity. Don't allow the perception of what we think death is to control how you experience it.

Go out and sit with the night sky. Then get up and live Life with dignity, peace, and love through all its infinite stages of change.

11.

CONSCIOUS
INCARNATION ONE

IT'S IMPOSSIBLE TO steer your way through Life. If you have your hands on the wheel of your Life, and you are trying to make your way somewhere, then you will have to learn by crashing. I say this because I have learned from crashing—a lot. So I recommend taking your hands off the wheel and letting Life/God steer. You will go through a lot less suffering.

This has everything to do with Conscious Incarnation but there are some important discussions that need to set the stage before I go deeply into this topic, which is the culmination of *The Practice*. But, because you are probably curious about this chapter's title, Conscious Incarnation means that you accept the potential that Life will, does, and can change infinitely—and you allow that truth to transform you. This has multiple implications for your life.

In an earlier chapter, I urged you to release emotions around such inevitable, but natural, events as death. But now, I'd like you to consider releasing emotions around your own natural death—the death of your physical form and the person you consider yourself to be. How do you come to terms not only with the death of your body, but with the death of *you* as a field of consciousness? How do you die with conscious awareness?

You—as your body, and you—as a field of consciousness, will go through an infinite number of changes throughout the eternal process that is Life. Haven't we changed many times since we were newborn babies? Yes, you and I will continue to change—eternally.

Life/Death are intertwined so much that we don't realize that death—in part—is what keeps us alive.

To begin, realize that how you perceptually and emotionally experience Life will directly affect how your *body* experiences Life. Thoughts of resistance and feelings of stress cause dis-ease, which will manifest in your body.

An example is my own resistance to letting go of being a doctor who provided chiropractic adjustments to being a doctor who was able to more fully become a spiritual teacher. My resistance to this change contributed to intense neck and arm pain. Yet, when I surrendered the part of me that was *attached* to being a chiropractic doctor and let that part of myself die, the neck and arm pain spontaneously resolved and has not returned since. I told you I've tried to steer my life and have had to learn though crashing. This is an example of how allowing necessary change resolves dis-ease and heals suffering. I could have continued to adjust patients until I had to quit because of the pain, but I chose to surrender into the truth more deeply; at that point, suffering was no longer necessary because when I removed my resistance to divine order the symptoms resolved immediately. Life thrives on divine order.

In a similar way, our emotions and feelings affect how our bodies experience death, including the bodily changes that occur or fail to occur, and how they occur. I will compare this kind of emotional and perceptual stance toward your own death to the intuitive approach that I recommend in *The Practice.* I hope it will give you a better understanding of how death is always with us, how it keeps us alive, and how accepting it leads to Conscious Incarnation and transformation.

First, let me briefly review the emotional stance toward our own death. From a young age, we're taught to fear death, but the truth is that we exist within Life and we rely on the force of death, in part, for our aliveness. Science has proven that every cell of our body dies and is replaced. We had to die to infancy to become a child, and die to childhood to become a teenager and die to adolescence to become adults. We rely on death to go on living. Therefore it behooves us to embrace all of Life, which includes the moment(s) of our own death(s).

As I studied in Life's classroom and developed my intuitive knowing, I began to sense that as well-intentioned as we may be about accepting death, our addiction to our emotions around it has kept us from transforming our consciousness as rapidly as we could. We are advancing at a slower rate than our potential will allow.

On a purely physical level, if you brush your arm with your hand, you have instantly killed 10,000 skin cells. You are not the same! Our bodies exemplify, on a microcosmic level, what is going on continuously in the Universe—a dying and a regenerating.

Our red blood cells live one hundred twenty days; every one hundred twenty days, our red blood cells—part of "us"—die and are regenerated—and as a result, so are we. Our organs too are constantly being regenerated. We know that cells within the organs only last a certain number of days or years and we know that we don't have the same cells in our bodies that we did when we were children.

Ask yourself why a person would be sick for a prolonged period in Life when the organs involved in the sickness would have regenerated—perhaps multiple times—during the timeframe of the sickness. By now, you know the answer: because we hold on. Because we don't allow ourselves to outgrow our emotional attachments to who we think we are. Our egocentric attachment to things in Life—even sickness (maybe especially sickness) keeps that energy of dis-ease present even in the new cells that are generated in the organs. Otherwise, we would outgrow sickness like we did when we were children.

Cellular memory is based on your past emotional experiences. Cells of themselves don't want to remember to be afraid or to live in fear. We imprint those emotional experiences on our cellular memory. And that memory is not only imprinted in the cells of our body, as cellular memory, it is also imprinted on our souls. Soul memory carries on from lifetime to lifetime.

Just because your cells die doesn't mean your soul memory dies. This is why past lifetimes can have a present physical symptom in our present lives because the energy around belief, emotions, and our opinions about Life continue to be stored in our soul memory.

I'll say it again, part of us goes on infinitely. It makes sense that Life goes on because God wants us to resolve— and Life encourages us to resolve—that dis-ease that is triggered by old emotional patterns, especially of fear. Let go of those fear patterns.

Unless you resist—Life will take these emotional patterns and beliefs from you. Life is always asking us to go to the places where we are scared, nervous, or worried, because those are the beliefs that keep us from growing in consciousness—those are the ones we must release. You can resist this process but when you resist, Life demands that *you* resolve the fear patterns. Too often, we don't allow ourselves to outgrow our emotions and the reactions they cause in us. We believe they are necessary to get through Life. We believe they are too necessary to let go, when truth be told they only cause us increased sickness and dis-ease.

I hope you understand now that your emotions and reactions are intimately involved in the dis-ease process, and they literally can be the seal of your own death. Emotions and feelings affect self chemistry. When dis-ease cells reproduce based on your emotional reactions or your opinions and judgments that are based on those emotional reactions, the cells hold on to the dis-ease that would otherwise naturally die, just as naturally as our skin cells or our red blood cells. But some people are very attached to what "should" be. Some people are very much attached to their own dis-ease, so much so that they refer to it as "my" disease. If our cells are continually being replaced, what is guiding the new cells to be sick? *We* are.

We can tell those cells to die—and they will die if we can let our emotions around the illness die. As we let ourselves die to what we *believe* is the truth about us, allowing ourselves to become more conscious, then those cells will be strengthened and guided by the higher consciousness. Tell any cells of dis-ease in you to die.

This is what I do: I help people die by bringing them into a new Conscious Incarnation of higher enlightenment that creates an order in the cells so that people can then heal spontaneously. I help people identify all the areas of their lives where they are stuck or hanging on, where their emotions are at work and their reactions are at work. I help them release those places where they are stuck. When they do release their emotions, their believed thoughts, and their consciousness around those thoughts, beliefs, and events, they make room for a higher level of consciousness to be born into their system. Once the lower level of consciousness disappears, which is what Life wants to happen, then that new, higher level of consciousness takes over and people experience what they think is a spontaneous healing. Something is gone—and they wonder how I did it! This is how.

Yet, I want to teach all people how to do spontaneous healing for themselves. It is not a trick. It is a truth. I use the force of Life, the force of birthing and the force of dying to heal people.

Many people consider physical death "beautiful" in the classic sense that death releases us from the feelings, thoughts, judgments, dis-ease, and sickness that we have been unable to release. So the assumption is that death, in this sense, transforms our suffering. But just because we die doesn't mean we necessarily transform! And death of the body does not mean death of the infinite consciousness.

Emotional energy will slow down transformation, which I'll discuss in the next chapter. You can always choose to experience your own or another's death emotionally like you've become used to. But, if you choose this way, remember that resistance breeds dis-ease so you may not have a pleasant time of it and neither will those around you.

Let's look at this topic one other way. We live in a society that generates friction and conflict on an ongoing basis. We navigate through Life, trying to avoid the friction and the conflict we ourselves created. Yet, some of us have found the truth through *engaging* in friction, conflict, death of form, and deterioration, while others of us have found the truth by *avoiding* friction and conflict. Let me say this a different way: Some of us have found health by avoiding sickness; others have found peace through war. All this time, for the most part, we have been gaining consciousness in an oppositional manner. We oppose Life in one way or the other. As a result, we are getting punitive "healing," so to speak. We are literally hurting ourselves, punishing ourselves to be healed. We have to be punished if we are to get better. We cannot get better without being punished.

Add to this our tribal nature—how we want to stick together, how we don't want to be alone or go out on the edge, how we want to fit in and not be too different—and you have all the ingredients for keeping your growth in consciousness to a rate within a standard deviation of normal range. This ensures that we aren't a "black sheep," that no one thinks we're crazy, and that we "fit in with the band."

That's why I keep saying that there is no personal choice! Take your hands off the wheel. Because you know and I know that given a personal choice, you and I will reflexively and instinctively hold on to those we love, those to whom we are emotionally attached. We will want to bring them along—even if they aren't yet ready. We will resist change so we can stay with them—because it's been our nature.

But if we don't resist and impede Life, which is always attempting to bring about the highest good of all—we won't need to be punished any longer.

It takes courage to become Consciously Incarnated. But Life will give you what you need to do it because Conscious Incarnation will increase the consciousness of all—and that is Life's purpose, the highest good for all.

So let's transform.

12.
CONSCIOUS
INCARNATION TWO

CONSCIOUS INCARNATION MEANS that you allow Life to birth and death you, moment to moment, according to the highest good. Think about it: Doesn't every moment have the potential to be a life-changing moment? Conscious Incarnation is an infinite practice.

In a nutshell, when we surrender to what is divinely ordered by Life, Life will resolve whatever it is that keeps us stuck. Truly, we are consciousness in human form—now.

Death is not one moment of your life, but every moment in your Life. At this point in *The Practice*, you know that in dealing with what keeps you stuck, the first step is to come to complete peace, acceptance. and love of Life, unconditionally.

This practice won't stop the "agi call it), so your body will still go changes. But, when you are at peace have dropped all resistance to the natural changes that occur, you will be peaceful with those changes and accept them as divinely guided by the order of Life, which is God.

As you come to terms with the natural changes in your body and feel peaceful with them, you will be led to no longer fear and resist the moment of your own death on a basic physical level. You will allow death to happen *naturally*. I am in no way condoning suicide for suicide's sake, because suicide has nothing to do with allowing death to happen naturally, as a part of Life.

Because death is not a one-time thing as our culture has taught us, I'm suggesting you not look at death as the end of your physical lifetime. Because it is not. See your death as nothing more than another moment in the process of Life. See it as an *ever-present* moment—a moment that brings about change—and these moments of change happen over and over again.

As you know, fear in your mind affects your body whether at the moment of death or before. Since death happens every moment—why fear? This truth is essential to accepting the divine course of your life and minimizing dis-ease.

We continually keep choosing to keep our "classic" self alive—instead of letting it constantly die and move on and die and move on. Begin practicing now and you will find your consciousness expanding more quickly—and that will spread to others around you. This is the foundation necessary for Conscious Incarnation.

So what does it mean to allow both your physical and

emotional form to change and then die—as Life sees fit?

There are signs. You will no longer be the person you seem to be now. Things you were certain about will change. Everything will seem different—and yet new. It's death's way of saying "That's over and done with."

And because you practice Conscious Incarnation in every moment, your life will have less suffering because you've allowed Life to naturally reduce your ignorance, and you've accepted your remaining ignorance completely. In a flash of a moment, you can transcend—that is, move beyond something that has kept you down. No longer do you need sickness or suffering or an inescapable life sentence to raise your consciousness. All that falls away when you stop resisting moment-by-moment dying. You will find yourself at peace. You may even find yourself loving and appreciating the momentary presence of death.

Practicing Conscious Incarnation cannot but transform your body into greater well-being. It cannot help but raise your consciousness and the consciousness of other beings as well. (All Life everywhere, on some level.) And not only on a spiritual level! The highest good is the highest good for the greatest number of beings, not only on a spiritual level, but in actual form—in actual being. Once you begin Conscious Incarnation, others will also have a greater opportunity to experience more health, love, and acceptance—simply because you are doing *The Practice*.

When we follow *The Practice*, we live in a relationship with Life that is neither encouraging nor discouraging of any aspect of the Life/Death process as it progresses naturally. We accept all of it. In doing so, we allow the Life/ Death process to become more efficient, thereby increasing the rate of transformation of all beings. Moreover we are no longer a prisoner of time, circumstance, or any belief or perception we may hold. They resolve, we let go. In this way, we assist in helping all of Life move into the greatest good.

To the extent you love and accept the moment of your death as having a purpose within Life, your acceptance of death will become a powerful force, enabling you to change more rapidly, to transform more easily. By "transform," I mean you will allow your form to change, which is the physical evidence of the spirit awakening. You will have many such changes. When your form is not happy, it's a sign that your spirit isn't happy. And when your spirit isn't happy, neither is your form. When you allow yourself to be in a space of love, peace, and acceptance and allow Life to bring you death and Life, Life will transform you—your form will change.

The body doesn't lie. In my opinion, God gave us bodies to enable us to see what we aren't able to see without them. We are a spiritual nature in a body because our spirit needs to be brought to a higher level of consciousness—and the body is the form God is using in our lifetime to show us when we are unconscious and where we are stuck. Truly, it is one of the miracles of the flesh—that it makes us conscious of what escapes our conscious awareness.

Death is neither the enemy of Life nor the opposite of Life. Death is the co-creative energy *within* Life. Life brings change and so does death. It's a marvelous balance.

As we move deeper in Conscious Incarnation, we more and more love and accept and be with Life. We don't carry around unresolved issues. We don't try to understand. We simply love and accept. We expend less energy as we allow Life to bring us into higher consciousness.

Here is another Truth: **The degree to which you unconditionally accept Life is proportional to your rate of transformation. And the degree to which you unconditionally accept Life is inversely proportional to the amount of dis-ease you will experience.**

Let change happen. To more and more fully experience the transformative power of Life, it is essential to embrace all the possibilities that Life may bring. As we surrender more deeply to all the possibilities of change—from a place of unconditional love without resistance—then we give Life a chance to affect us without unnecessary dis-ease, with less dis-ease created by our resistance.

When we keep ourselves alive in a space of sickness, it means we are attached to being what we believe we are; we keep ourselves alive even though our form is sick, even though it isn't working. This is a clear sign that we are back to believing in free will, that we keep alive our suffering even though that energy could be better used for the greater good.

There will still be signs of physical illness because a certain amount is necessary for growth in consciousness. I mentioned my own experience with neck and arm pain, which told me something about my resistance. That turned out to be necessary for my growing consciousness.

It helped me understand my spirit and what it needed. It was my Life instruction that we can eliminate all *unnecessary* illness by not resisting Life and its marvelous order. Life's changes are inevitable anyway. Let's get out of our own way and let change happen. Life and Death bring change. There is no day that we don't die and no moment we don't die, on some level.

As I said in the last chapter, death of the physical body is not a failsafe manner of transformation. Death cannot be transformational unless Conscious Incarnation has been practiced in Life. By this I mean that in order for transformation to occur, a sense of peace must envelop the body before and during the moment of death. The more peace that is present, the greater the degree of transformation. The more you practice this in the moments of your life before death, the more your death will transform you.

When you have a full conscious awareness of death—not only in your mind but also in your body—and that awareness is not impeded by fear or doubt, then your own naturally occurring death can bring spontaneous closure and resolution where needed. Because you have practiced Conscious Incarnation during the moments of your life that preceded the death of your body, Life, through death, will effortlessly remove your unconsciousness and allow higher consciousness to arise.

Transformation at the moment of death, per se, can only happen to its fullest extent if you realize and accept that death is not a once-in-a-lifetime occurrence. You see that death is a presence every moment as well as a moment-by-moment naturally occurring option.

Another benefit of Conscious Incarnation is that when we no longer fear and resist the moment of our own death, our soul memory can no longer affect our cells with dis-ease in this lifetime (and throughout the eternal process of Life.) By practicing in this lifetime, you may still have some physical illness left. But since Life is infinite you can practice again in your next form—with even fewer opportunities for dis-ease. At some future point, you will have no resistance left, no dis-ease, no form.

Remember, Life is dedicated to the sole purpose of transforming our unconsciousness into a higher consciousness. So when you allow Life to steer, what happens? No fear, no dis-ease, and higher consciousness. This is Conscious Incarnation.

It is not unreasonable to expect that as we transform, we can expect multiple lifetimes of enlightenment—not in a different body but within a single, ever-changing physical form. I call this process Conscious Incarnation. Enlightenment can happen in a single moment and it can happen in a momentary form. As a Life form, we are momentary. When you look at the age of the universe we are here for but a moment. If there is any doubt, consider the lifetime of a human being compared to the lifetime of the universe.

As you move deeper into Conscious Incarnation, you will understand that you don't *do* anything to make it happen. A healthy absence of self allows the absence of dis-ease because without ego, you don't see Life as something happening *to* you. You don't judge it. You just watch it happen. This is seeing Life through God's eyes. Then we no longer see ourselves as separate from God. The illusion of separateness from God is what separates us from God. We cannot be separated from God for we are in Life.

You also won't engage all that emotional energy around death and dying that you are so used to, because you will understand that emotions are unsustainable if you want to grow in conscious awareness and allow Life to transform your own ignorance and unconsciousness.

Conscious Incarnation means you become conscious in the flesh; consciousness defines our flesh, our bodies. You are no longer a prisoner of your flesh—don't blame the flesh! You are a prisoner only of the limitations you place on the possibilities of Life and what it can bring and how it can change. That is what makes you a prisoner of restrictions you impose on your body and on the conscious ability of the body to change—which it will do infinitely. You don't have to be a *slave* to something until you die or be a *prisoner* of something until you die or be *sick* until you die.

If you are still on the fence about this, consult your intuition and ask yourself: What choice is in the highest good? Is it an ongoing emotional experience that will inevitably contribute to increased suffering and sickness and sabotage enlightenment for me and for everyone else? Or is it practicing living in a way that embraces consciousness and welcomes enlightenment, a way that benefits me and everyone else as it relieves suffering and sickness? What answer does your intuition give you?

When Life can do its thing and meet with no resistance from you, then you will become "new" at a faster pace. "New" because at every possible moment, you will practice releasing any and all resistance. "New" because you've learned that resistance brings dis-ease, sickness, and suffering—and you've surrendered the personal choice to have dis-ease and sickness in this moment or in the moments that follow.

As you transform, this "new" you will lose its need to "understand," to know "why," and to survive. The new you will love more and more from an intuitive knowing, easily releasing emotions because you've seen the truth of the suffering they've caused.

When we surrender to Conscious Incarnation, we don't resist at all. We also don't understand and we don't judge. We let it all be as it is. Moment to moment, we die to our need to change anything *except* our acceptance of change.

At times, you'll surely have to walk this journey alone. But never forget that there are other beings who *are* with you in community; they have the same point of focus as you do and you can walk together in that space of acceptance whether it is in bodily form or in conscious awareness.

Don't have an expectation of what your life is supposed to be. Don't have an expectation of anything or anyone. Don't expect your wife or your husband to walk this path of greater consciousness with you. Don't expect your kids to. Maybe no one will come with you. On a daily basis, though, most of us aren't surrounded by people who walk with Conscious Incarnation as a focus. To embrace the Life/Death process and Conscious Incarnation is completely contrary to what most people do, to what most people believe, and to how most people live. What to do?

You probably already know: let go and accept. Let the feelings you have about other people die, whether they are walking with you focused on Conscious Incarnation or not. Be at peace with the fact that many people around you will continue to learn the same way they have always learned—the hard way; you will have to watch them suffer. So be it. Have unconditional compassion for them but allow them to suffer as long as they need to. As I've said, there are many ways to grow in consciousness, and suffering is one of them. If people have to bounce off the bumpers of Life, crash, and suffer, then that's what some people have to do. You might prefer to learn that way too, even as you engage in *The Practice*. Yet, if you stick with *The Practice*, you will move past the need to learn through suffering.

We don't *try*, We don't make a lot of effort. Conscious Incarnation and the potential for an acceleration in consciousness happens not because of effort but because of surrender, because we release our ingrained resistance. We focus on our internal development as the natural path to enlightenment. We release the external, go within, cultivate deep inner peace, love, and acceptance. Only then can we experience the outer reality through the inner developed consciousness.

The Practice (and Conscious Incarnation) is about being who you are, in a surrendered place of greatest enlightenment. It is about sharing your enlightenment with others whom Life brings to you—without trying to convert them. Practice having no expectations of the effect your own enlightenment will have on others. Surrender completely to the force of creation and to its source, God.

Begin to practice these teachings and you will find your own consciousness expanding more quickly. This expanding consciousness will spread to others around you. It will also become painfully obvious if you cannot let go of something or someone—and then you can practice some more. Because you've practiced for a while now, you will immediately know what to do: Consciously surrender all relationships with all people and things. Allow Life to show you where you need to go or where things need to go or where others need to be. Wherever Life takes you or others is just fine. You die every moment—and you remember this.

There is no right and wrong, no good or bad when it comes to Conscious Incarnation. Resist for awhile and grow more conscious at a slower rate. The resistance will eventually wear down and you will become ready to relax into the truth of Life's divine order. Move ahead quickly in *The Practice* and grow more conscious at a faster rate and affect the growth of consciousness in others, too.

As you practice, practice will become as natural as breathing. It will take less energy and concentration. But until then, you may find yourself "working" at remembering that Life and Death may await you—both of them in the very next moment and the moment after that. And then you decide to live your life like this—at the edge where Life or Death could take you at any moment. And you will not resist.

As we allow Life to teach us and to change us—on its terms, in its way, in its time, we notice that we are happier and more peaceful. One day, we notice that there is far less suffering in our lives, and we smile. We don't need to generate all that angst and energy any more—and as a result we grow in consciousness. We become an Incarnation of Consciousness.

The effect of your growing consciousness is for the highest good for all. If you are experiencing a level of success in doing *The Practice,* trust me—you have nothing to be concerned about, whether it is your own life or the lives of those around you. You will naturally find yourself in the appropriate places. You will naturally find yourself having the appropriate conversations. You will find that your job, your family, your career, are going exactly where they are supposed to go. You will find that all is well not because your hands are *on* the wheel, but because they are *off.*

At this level of Conscious Incarnation, *The Practice* shows you how incredibly consumed you have been with the emotional experiences of your life, your external experiences, and how they have indeed limited the rate of transformation of your consciousness, and kept you, your body, and—to some degree those around you—in a state of dis-ease. Your dedication to *The Practice* will increase the unveiling of your God-given inner potential by removing what obstructs it. All you have to do—as we all know—is practice.

I became proficient at experiencing Life in the way I set forward here because I practiced. As a student in Life's classroom, I have come to know that this is the only way to experience Life truly, in its purest form—as a reflection of God.

Think of yourself as a reflection of Life witnessing yourself being a reflection of Life. It's a most amazing experience. Eventually, living Life full and loving it unconditionally will be effortless—sometimes, then all the time, in any and every situation. Life then becomes an eternal experience happening moment to moment.

As you practice, you become free—as Life always intended you to be. Practice for yourself. Practice for your loved ones. Practice for the world, for all of Life everywhere.

ONE WITHIN
THE ONE

THE ETERNAL PURPOSE of the continual practice of living Life fully and loving Life unconditionally is to allow—and then cultivate—a Life experience in which your own life, including what you considered yourself to be, slowly dies away. What remains is God energy.

This God-energy manifests in an ever-changing form that is the "new" you. The new you is no longer governed by all the data from perceptual experience or by your unconscious. Neither is it any longer governed by the unconscious opinion of others or by the institutions they have created. The new you as a field of Life is governed only by the law of the highest good based on unconditional love, acceptance, and peace, and compassion, which is the true law of God.

Life allows an infinite number of life forms to exist and evolve simultaneously;

- All have the perfect experience necessary for the evolution and transformation of unconsciousness into a higher field of relative consciousness.
- All happens in a state of complete order and harmony; whether we perceive it or not. Even though we are beset with our constant ignorant resistance, Life is eternally patient—beyond our comprehension.
- An order that we can observe and appreciate in Nature is the nature of Life.
- This order is not hidden but is completely obvious and out in the open when we look at Life with Life's eye, through intuitive knowing, through the eye of unconditional love, acceptance, and peace. Through the Eye of God.
- The purpose of Life is nothing other than an eternal choice-less surrender into an unconditionally loving relationship with *The Practice* of Life.

Never again do you need to concern yourself with the outer influences of this world, or try desperately to accommodate all its never-ending needs and desires. Nothing quenches your desire any more except *The Practice* of Life. You've given up the endless attempts to find happiness in superficial temporal pleasure that cannot withstand the eternal test of Life or provide any kind of peace. You dedicate yourself to living fully and loving Life unconditionally for eternity. You've taken your hands off the steering wheel of Life and you feel free.

What anyone thinks about you or your practice of living and loving Life is of no importance to you; the opinions of others are irrelevant. You practice for yourself and for the highest good of everyone else in a space of unconditional love and gratitude. You practice for Life itself, for the unconditional love of God to which you have bowed in choice-less surrender for all eternity. It is all you need to know.

The perceptual events of this world no longer control you or you them. They do not dictate who you will be, who you've been, or who you will become. You let everything go, release it all, in an act of choice-less surrender. You are in this world, but no longer *of* it. You live in an inner space full of peace. You are at peace with all possible outcomes of Life. Each day you grow more peaceful with every opportunity Life brings you. You encounter any one of an infinite number of possibilities with peace, joy, and trust.

You realize that you are part of Mystery and you embrace Mystery. You feel eternally grateful for the wisdom Life bestows upon you. Your whole being is open to whatever Life/God brings. You suppress nothing, yet your emotions and the emotions of others no longer control you.

You are free to be and do whatever Life asks, free to serve Life in whatever way you are instructed, from one moment to another. You have a bodily form yet, relatively speaking, you are undefined. You are everything and nothing—all at once.

You are everything God asks of you. You are ready to serve the great master of all eternity. As infinite potential, you are ready for miracles to come through you. You are limitless and unbounded. You are one with all those around you, those you are aware of and those you are not. As a child incarnate, you are one with the universe for all eternity.

Now, it is enough for you to be present and prepared to love unconditionally. You no longer need to fix anyone or anything. As a result, you bring peace wherever you go.

You no longer need to judge anything or anyone. Your only tool is unconditional love and acceptance for all parts of yourself and everyone else. And it is enough.

Compassion is the only state of being you will have available when you see others resisting Life's divine order. Yet, you won't blame them for "getting in their own way." Feeling "bad" is no longer in the highest good, and feeling good is always a result of balance.

Death is a momentary occurrence that you love and embrace, allow and accept. As you let go of loved ones, you accept the truth that Life and Death happen every moment, eternally.

Karma fades into Forgiveness, and Forgiveness morphs into unconditional acceptance in the moment.

Evil becomes obsolete because it is nothing more than unconsciousness and ignorance in disguise. You recognize them as an amazing opportunity for growth in conscious awareness and a dependence on God's divine order and grace.

Life becomes an opportunity to experience everything in a space of complete peace, love, and acceptance. In this place of deeper and deeper peace and surrender, you become the infinite peaceful observer of

God's divine order. You become a spectator to the greatest miracle of creation: Life.

For more information on Dr. Keith Jordan
visit all or any of the following websites:

www.DrKeithJordan.com

www.OWCenter.com

www.GoodnRaw.com

www.TheCommunityOfOne.com

Or contact his wellness center:

Optimal Wellness Center
11860 Clifton Blvd.
Lakewood, OH 44107
216-521-2225

Made in the USA
Lexington, KY
30 January 2012